PORCH STORIES

Dr. Rev. Larry Macon Sr.
Brother of
Ray Macon Sr.

OTHER BOOKS
by Dr. Larry L. Macon, Sr.

The Black Church at Its Best

Discipling African American Males

Messages for Modern Times

Then They Shall Fast

Beware of Those Cover Ups

PORCH STORIES

Told and Interpreted

LARRY L. MACON, SR.

with

DANIEL L. MACON
and LARRY L. MACON, JR.

Porch Stories: Told and Interpreted
by Larry L. Macon, Sr.
with Daniel L. Macon and Larry L. Macon, Jr.

© Copyright 2010

SAINT PAUL PRESS, DALLAS, TEXAS

First Printing, 2010

The name SAINT PAUL PRESS and its logo are registered as a trademark in the U.S. patent office.

ISBN-13: 978-0-9827966-6-5

Printed in the U.S.A.

Dedicated to my father, Louis Macon,
and my mother, Delina Macon,
who have gone to be with the Lord.

And to my six brothers and two sisters:
Richard, Walter, Robert, Philip,
Raymond, Elmer, Geraldine, and Helen.

CONTENTS

PART IV: IS JUSTICE JUST FOR US?

PART V: WHEN THE LORD IS INVOLVED

BY MARILYN MACON

Well, Pastor Macon, you are Mt Zion's
starting quarterback,
Determined to lead us to victory in Christ Jesus!
You're not a second string quarterback waiting on the
sidelines to be put in the game;
No, you were placed in this game thirty years ago
a quarterback for Mt. Zion.
God is your coach, the Bible is your game plan,
the Holy Spirit is your uniform
And you have thrown the football to us
time and time again.
As players on your team
you have given us your vision – the game plan –
for this church
And you have taught and preached how to stir up the gift
Sometimes we need a tailback or a fullback
to push our way through

Or a strong safety or a cornerback to intervene—
a linebacker surely helps out,
And a wide receiver to catch those long passes
you sometimes throw out;
Some guards and some right and left tacklers
are pretty important too.
Can't you just imagine their job trying to block and keep
the enemy from getting through.
We also need some special teams,
the kickers and punters too
Standing by just in case you need their special expertise.
And I am most happy to report,
even though every game is not won,
We have made some touchdowns
and won three Super Bowls.
In 1985, when we built the Octagon Church,
You won a Super bowl and the Coach was quite pleased.
And next, in 2002, when we built the New Worship Center,
That's Super Bowl two and the Coach
was very happy with you.
And next, in 2007, you took us to Heaven with
a brand new Fine Arts Center.
That's Super Bowl three and the Head Coach
was ecstatic with you.
We're headed to the Super Bowl once more
as we continue phase four of your vision.
And I'm sure we shall win Super Bowl four,
with God as your Coach and your quarterback skills.
In closing we say, we love you and we admire your
determination and faith in God.

PREFACE

THE PORCH STORIES INSTILLED
IN ME FROM CHILDHOOD

The love of stories was instilled in me as a very young child. I was born into a large Northern black family in Cincinnati, Ohio, that retained a black Southern culture. Most African Americans who came to Cincinnati from the South during post-slavery days declared their freedom from Southern racist culture once they crossed the Ohio River from Kentucky and accepted a Northern non-racist culture. However, most retained their rich Southern culture of family and heritage. My family was one of them, through my father, Louis Macon, who filled every day in the evenings telling stories on the front porch that centered around his southern heritage in Alabama. It became a tradition in our family to hear those many stories. There was not a family gathering without those marvelous tales and narratives created out of this mastermind patriarch who walked this world for over eight decades.

I spent untold hours as a child sitting in my father's room, late at night, on the floor listening to either his many conversations with my mother about his experience in the South, or listening to tapes of sermons he'd made of early black church services in the 1960's.

The posture of the early preacher was to deliver narrative sermons and I was quite overcome by these messages heard in the traditional black Baptist church. All of these influences created in me a lifelong affection for the story form of truth, a fondness that drew me to create, what I believe, moving collections of narratives that I have entitled *Porch Stories*, which is also porch theology. The theology especially comes to life in this book through stories and messages by my sons, Larry Jr., and Daniel, as well as myself.

The formulation of this book was a genuine collaboration with my sons, Larry L. Macon, Jr., and Daniel Macon who encouraged me to do some writing during this time in my life. I invited them to join me on this journey. They thoughtfully and carefully helped me restate and clarify sentence after sentence and thought after thought in many of the stories. It would not be an overstatement to describe them as the co-authors of this book, for without their work, this would be an entirely different set of stories. Their interest and encouragement, not only in this book, but also in my life, are clearly the greatest graces I have ever known, and all that they are and have done for me are beyond my powers of expression to thank them. The additions to the porch stories told by them are most valuable. In Larry's studies during law school, he became fascinated by some of the issues of justice and wanted to explore them and we have added some of these stories and interpretative paradigms that might be told on the porch to families who would want to explore the subject of equality.

The three of us are also deeply indebted to Marilyn, my most beautiful wife and long-term partner. She is a real encourager and was the first one to read these stories. Yet, Larry Jr's., lawyerly mind as a graduate of the inaugural class of the historic FAMU (Florida Agricultural and Mechanical University) Law School in Florida has been an added value.

I cannot thank Daniel, my younger son enough, who recently graduated from Bowling Green State University. As children both of my sons allowed me to re-tell some of these porch stories on the front porch of our home, as they were growing up. I embellished the stories as I told them to my sons. Also, I am thankful to my daughter-in-law, Elodie, who has been more like a daughter to me. She has brought forth our next generation of hearers of porch stories: Alana Maria Macon and Michael Lawrence Macon. Hopefully and prayerfully, our next generation will not only be hearing these porch stories, but in decades to come, will be telling them and creating others.

Last, I am indebted to people around me who have remained faithful in their words of wisdom and for showing me the art of telling stories. They are my senior pastor, Rev.

Dr. Henry J. Payden, Sr., Pastor Emeritus of the historic Holy Trinity Baptist Church in Cleveland; my colleague, Dr. C. Jay Matthews; my close friend, Emery Ivery and his lovely wife, Annette, who have always been there for me, starting from elementary school, college and even now; and to Rev. Dr. Otis Moss, Jr., and Rev. Dr. Marvin A. McMickle, both of Cleveland, Ohio, for their continued support and friendship as clergy mentors. Not withstanding, I cannot say enough for the pastor who mentored me as a child, the late Rev. Dr. Bennett W. Smith, who is the former pastor of the First Baptist Church of Mt. Auburn in Cincinnati, Ohio. He was also the former president of the National Progressive Baptist Convention (PNBC). There was never a Sunday at the First Baptist Church of Mt. Auburn in Cincinnati, Ohio, that I was not totally engrossed with his preaching style and mannerisms as a child.

I will always be thankful for the two professors who held me in safekeeping during my doctoral program at Ashland Theological Seminary: the Rev. Dr. William H. Myers and Rev. Dr. Douglas Little, who constantly challenged my thinking and praxis. I am also indebted to the Religious Studies Department at Cleveland State University, where for the past fifteen years, I have taught black religious courses. This has enabled me to not only gain an understanding of the black church, but also an appreciation for black heritage.

Also, I am grateful to the best and greatest congregation in the world that has allowed me to mature over these past thirty years and never wavered from my direction as their pastor, and that is the Mt. Zion Church of Oakwood Village, Ohio. This church, with its more than 6,000 members and mega-church complex, has never ceased to give me their support as their pastor. They are truly some of the nicest people in the world and have always followed my vision. God has manifested this vision in more ways than one over the years through its ministry.

Most of all, I thank my God through our Lord and Savior Jesus Christ, who affirms my belief that our stories are really His stories being unfolded in unique forms and *kairos* moments of life. I pray that all who read these stories would take moments in life to pause and reminisce over their rich heritage and share their porch stories that God has given them. I challenge each of you to remember that each of us has at least one marvelous porch story to tell and now is the time to tell it!

—Dr. Larry Macon, Sr.,
Senior Pastor
Mt. Zion Church of Oakwood Village

INTRODUCTION

THE HOUSE IS ON FIRE
THE HARDEST TIME IN MY LIFE

After my father died in a terrible house fire accident, the hardest event in my life was seeing him taken out of the house from the side door past the front porch. He would never return to the front porch where many of the porch stories were told.

Thereafter, I promised myself that I would write this book with my sons in memory of both my father and mother. I had already written several books, namely: *Discipling African American Men: How to Get Black Men Into Church and Keep Them There; Messages for Modern Times,* which gives several inspirational sermons to the church community by leading pastors in the Greater Cleveland area who led some of the most historic and amazing churches in the city; *Then They Shall Fast,* which is a book of personal empowerment for the community of faith; *Beware of Those Cover Ups,* a book to help people expose sin in their lives and the necessary corrections to become a part of victorious living; and *The Black Church At Its Best,* my latest book, which looks at African-American religions. I have now decided to add this important writing to my collection. This latter work emanates from my own teaching at the Cleveland State University in Ohio for the past fifteen years. Hence, I thought it was time that I wrote *Porch Stories* with each of them ending with an interpretation or reflection that can be applicable to life.

I wanted to present a miniature form of my autobiography in a unique and different format through these several short stories. However, the reader needs to know that some of these porch stories are *true* and were actually told by my father, Louis Macon, who has gone to be with the Lord in Heaven, where my mother, Delina Macon, joins him. She too, sat on the porch with us. Others of them are not true stories but are made up or embellished out of my creative mind. These were told by me to my children, Larry Jr. and Daniel, both ministers of the gospel, while their mother, Marilyn, listened on. Still, others of them are *almost true* and are at best, memories. I take no credit for their originality; only God is truly original, the rest of us are simply passing on to others what we have first received. Other family members could have told some of the stories to me. I can't really recall. Others are stories told and interpreted by my sons.

Moreover, others of these porch stories are *definitely* untrue, though because of the way in which they are presented they sound as if they could be true. It's all up to the reader to decide on which story is true, almost true, and *definitely* not true. It all becomes a part of your personal journey with us. Your ultimate conclusions as to the many points and thoughts to these stories are attempts to relay, reveal, and raise issues about life itself. In other words, the reader will create his or her own reality in reading and interpreting these stories that may cause you, the reader, to move forward with your own thoughts.

Hopefully, all who read these stories, sometimes told in the late twentieth century dialect, will receive a renewal of spirit and thoughts that will help you pick up on a rich tradition in African-American families. Also, other family traditions from other ethnic backgrounds will be appreciated.

The porch, that small area built at either the front, back or side of many Southern and Northern homes held deep secrets and meaningful family life. If it was left up to me I would suggest that we never build another house without a large open front porch. This has been the place where empowerment for the family has been achieved and a network of family-hood has been strengthened in a day where the breakdown of almost half of every two-parent household has been occurring. I believe communities and neighborhoods could become a brotherhood and sisterhood, if we would only learn again the art of telling our stories on the front porch and passing them on from one generation to the next.

May you be blessed, as I have been in creating and interpreting these porch stories that have been and will continue to be sent down from generation to generation. May God richly bless you as you read these porch stories.

PART ONE

THE TEACHER

THE TEACHER

OUR GREATEST TEACHERS light a fire in our souls that burn for a lifetime. They motivate us to learn more, reach higher and reach beyond the capacity of our circumstances. They relive their own dreams through the accomplishments of their students who believe their lessons and aspire to their vision.

Louis Macon, my father, was one such teacher. He showed me the strong thread that ran through our culture as a proud family of African-American decent who believed and trusted in the Bible, the church, the family, and the community. He gave me a love for parenthood and siblinghood, as well as, for the preaching and teaching of the Scriptures. He taught me to look for heroes in our history who had transformative powers. He instilled in me a hatred for that which was not right and a love for truth and justice through stories. He was my teacher in life and for life. I am now a teacher because of him.

Delina Macon, my mother, motivated me to rise above insurmountable obstacles through listening to my father's porch stories. She believed in her husband and the father of her children. She, too, introduced me to a new world, as she made me sit on the porch and listen intently to the many stories told. She knew he was speaking truth to power. My father's teaching style and my mother's supportive style motivated me to become a story-tclling minister and writer. I am a writer of porch stories because of them. My sons are writers of porch stories because of this teacher.

THE CHURCH AT ITS BEST
An Experience that is Unforgettable

CHAPTER 1

Not forsaking the assembling of ourselves together, as is the manner of some, but exhorting one another, and so much the more as you see the day approaching (Hebrews 10:25).

It's Saturday night in the Queen City of Cincinnati, Ohio, and mother has asked all nine of her children to get ready for church the next day, Sunday. The lights are on throughout the house and the water in the bathtub is running. All the while I can smell the dinner being cooked in the kitchen—green beans and ham, fried chicken, smothered potatoes, and yes, the peach cobbler pies. We were getting ready for the big event of the week—going to the black church, which was the neighborhood church in the area. We couldn't wait to meet and greet all of our young friends, the mothers of the church, the army-like lead ushers, and the line of men deacons. Yet, the central figure in the historic black church and at our family church was the preacher and pastor, Rev. Bennett W. Smith, who entered in church with his long entourage of ministers and deacons.

Sunday morning has just arrived and all the children are whisked off to the bathroom to relieve themselves and quickly wash up and put on their Sunday clothes. The Sunday clothes were those special pants, shirts, socks, and shoes that could only be worn on Sundays. The breakfast has been prepared with the aroma of bacon, fried potatoes, eggs, and homemade biscuits made by my father, Chairman of the Deacon Board, Louis J. Macon. We are prepared to ride to church in shifts since there are so many of us, with the youngest of the siblings leading off the first shift so they can also attend Sunday school on time.

Going to church was not a chore or ritual, but more so a spiritual journey from start to finish. All of the children had to attend Sunday school. It was exciting because Sunday school for children was held in the same sanctuary area as adult Sunday school. In the adult class, my father was usually the Sunday school teacher and chief debater, arguing his points whether they were right or wrong, and using the intonation of a man in authority to convince his hearers that his points were always valid and were to be accepted by virtue of his position in the church. This authoritative tone was most exciting to us youngsters who overheard him teach.

Although Dad did not have a high school diploma or even a complete elementary education (he only graduated from the third grade in a one-room school from the nearby burroughs of Opelika, Alabama), Dad always had a convincing and compelling theological slant and argument. My father could not even write his own name when he joined the U. S. Army and wrote an X next to his name that the recruiter signed in his stead. In fact, he was born LJ Macon and because the recruiter could not accept an initial as a name, Dad was smart enough to declare the initials meant Louis James. From that day on, instead of being called LJ, he was known as Louis James, but later dropped the James and became known as Louis. He really learned how to read and write through an army buddy who committed to helping this young sixteen-year-old black male, who looked more like a young army colonel, to read and write. Dad was six feet, two inches tall, had jet black wavy hair, a light complexion—being half-white, half-black and part Cherokee Indian, he would proudly proclaim.

It was this mixed black man who I saw on Sunday morning with his beautiful wife, Delina, from Hazard, Kentucky. He often told us how they met. He drove a truck with a friend up North and stopped for a minute in Hazard to eat at one of the local Negro restaurants, only to discover one of the finest young black women in the town. She was only seventeen years of age and the daughter of a coal miner from a large family. Dad eyed her, approached her, and proposed marriage to her. After giving her a kiss, though she was already dating one of the local boys in the community, my dad promised to return to the area within two weeks to make his intention known to her father. After all, she was not twenty-one and needed her father's written permission to sign off on the marriage license. Though Dad often boasted about not caring whether her father signed off or not, he was going to marry this beautiful, long black-haired, light-skinned girl named Delina. Without reluctance, her father consented to the marriage and Louis and Delina were married and off to the bright lights of Cincinnati where, within ten years, they had nine children—seven boys and two girls, who they would make sure grew up in church.

It was on Sundays that the journey started with the awakening to a new day, a line to the one bathroom on Bodman Avenue in Cincinnati, a drive to the First Baptist Church that stood on top of the highest hill in Cincinnati, overlooking the beautiful city and the parade of familiar faces in church. There was Deacon Collier, a tall dark-skinned man who was known as the whooping and singsong praying deacon, one who could always out-yell the chairman, my father. There was old Mother Fuse who always walked into church with her fox fur, even in the summer. My brothers and I could not wait until she lay the fur over the back of the church pew with the small fox head protruding towards us; we could play with it without her knowing. And then there was the fussy old usher, Ms. Kimble, who was always threatening to tell our mother, the lovely Deaconess Delina, of our misbehaviors of the day. It was almost as if she gloried in making our lives miserable. In fact, unknown to our mother and father, we would follow her home on occasion and throw mud balls or snowballs at her door when she went into the house after making her Sunday report to our parents, who, by the way, usually overlooked much of what she said or wrote.

And then, there was the first family of the church, Rev. and Mrs. Bennett W. Smith, who both were young and attractive, having two children at the time. He too, as my dad, grew up in Alabama near my father's hometown, neither one of them knowing their father, and the two of them claimed some kind of special silent brotherhood. Also, I cannot overlook how attractive his wife was and how the Macon and Smith families appeared to be two of the finest looking families in church.

It was right after Sunday school, going into morning worship, that church became more than an event. The seven deacons would stand before the congregation with their strong masculine faces, dark suits, white shirts, and matching ties. Their shoes were always highly shined and their socks were either black or white. The musician was usually at rest at the piano, yet ready to chime in on a tune during the deacons' prayers. But old Deacon Collier, along with Deacon Sullivan, would ring out with one of those historic Dr. Watts' hymns, "I love the Lord, He heard my cry." However, no one could quite beat the pastor, Rev. Bennett W. Smith, who, with his bass, baritone, and sometimes beautiful tenor voice, would enter from the back of the small framed church and take over the hymns and songs while walking towards the front with his entourage of ministers. The choir would then follow them with the swaying movement of one of the finest choirs in Cincinnati. Ms. Fuse had found her seat, though she would always walk down the aisle a little late so the people could glory in her fashion and fur. People would rush in on another entrance aisle to take their places and one would have thought that the millennium had just been ushered into the midst of a holy and sacred moment.

Once the choir reached the choir stand in the front of the church and the pianist/organist set the tone, there were exultant shouts of, "Praise the Lord." "Amen." "Hallelujah." "Sing it, choir." This has been historically termed the call and response in the black church. After the singing and soloists emotionally moved the congregation into times of joy and praise, it was time for the offering. The offertory time of giving was never my moment. After all, I had to give the five cents given to me by my mother for church, which to me could have had better used at the local candy store. But, of course, Mom would always look around and check to see if all of her children placed their Sunday morning money into the offering tray. Afterwards, the exciting setting regained momentum when the pastor stood in front of the large wooden pulpit or podium and again struck up a song. The deacons would stand, the choir would sing, and the women, especially the older women, would shout to the point of fainting.

I remember on one occasion, as I came up the stairs after relieving myself in the downstairs restroom, how my father and young Deacon Sullivan were carrying a woman out of the church and down the steps to help her regain consciousness. In observing her strange mannerism of unconsciousness, I noticed that she held a tight grip onto her purse, as she was about to be carried down the steep steps. I heard my father tell her softly, yet authoritatively, "Sister, you are awfully heavy (she was), so, if you shake too hard we are going to drop you down these steps." I noticed she remained very still from that point on. Of course, my father later on explained how the woman loved to be carried down the steps by these young, handsome deacons.

Dad would return to the service and the excitement of the day, and the preaching by Rev. Smith, who had already shouted the people from the singing of hymns. It was time for the preached word. And to be honest, I as a young person, never really understood a word Pastor Smith said because most of the time he would sort of whoop, grump, and gasp for breath after each word or phrase and then at the moment of the climax in the sermon, he would repeatedly clear his throat, moan and groan, sing-song his sermon ending and then yell. It was on then! There would not be a person sitting, even us young children, and there would not be a dry eye in the church. Members, both men and women, would fall out, yell, scream, and shout and when the invitation to become a Christian would occur, there was always someone going to the front to join the church. On one occasion, it was wine-head Willy, who I witnessed being drunk on Saturday nights down at the

local lounge near our home. Or it was dice-shooting Bob who
would be near the neighborhood bar located up the street
from the church. Or Ms. Prissy, the late night streetwalker,
who would run to the front to be saved.

LIFE LESSONS YOU CAN TAKE AWAY
FROM THIS STORY

As a youngster, all this mystified me, especially since I
was not able to articulate or analyze it. Yet, at the same time, it
thrilled me and excited my very soul. What then was it that
occurred on Sunday mornings on the top of Sycamore Hill,
the highest point in Cincinnati? I think now, after many years
of research and teaching black religion in America at
Cleveland State University, and preaching for more than a
quarter of a century at Mt. Zion Church of Oakwood Village,
and with over forty years of experience as a minister in several
black churches, that this was *the black church at its best!*

W. E. B. Dubois, a scholar, writer, and activist in the
defense of the human dignity of black people, in his writings
Of the Faith of the Fathers, reported that the religion of black
people centered on the preacher, the music, and the outward
expressiveness of blacks. To Dubois, the preacher was the
most unique personality developed by the Negro on
American soil because the preacher became the leader, a
politician, an orator, and a "boss." E. Franklin Frazier tells
us that the preacher who felt called by God had to be able to

preach rather than have a lot of instruction in the Christian faith. In fact, Frazier, in his book, *Negro Church in America*, gives the qualifications of the black preacher.

Frazier said that the traditional black preacher had to be able to first, "Tell the story." This is to suggest that he had to be able to use great imagery in his sermon. He had to be able to make his hearer see the picture so plainly until the dialog that went on included affirmation from the congregation in responses like "Paint the picture," "I see what you are saying," and "Press your point." There have been those who have heard black preaching about the fires of hell, who have reported that after the preacher gave a sermon on hell, they could literally see the flames and smell the smoke. Also, the preacher had to be able to sing the sacred songs called Spirituals with a sort of moaning. Much of the earlier black church prayers, reading of scripture, and testifying were with a kind of singing and moaning expression. Furthermore, the historic black preacher had to shout the slave into holy dancing. Last, the slave preacher had to exhibit leadership capabilities. He had to be able to direct his followers. And as most scholars would argue, church then became *church!*

Presently, the black Baptist church is a rich and exciting experience, which emphasizes warm and intimate relationships. This denominational church has strengthened both the soul and spirit of its worshippers. Today, one can still find traditional worship within this denomination. At any convention there is an effort by the choir, singers, and preacher to shout the congregation through the traditional style of worship with the excitement of a whooping, sing-song preacher. There is much dialog going on as a response and call to the message and service by way of loud "Amens," "Praise the Lords" and so forth. The preacher remains the central figure in the church, with singing seen as second to preaching. One can still hear such traditional songs and spirituals such as "Go Down Moses" and "Roll, Jordan, Roll." One can find songs being sung by soloists such as "Precious Lord," created by the father of gospel music, Thomas Dorsey.

THE LIT-UP CHURCH
The Spirits in the Light

CHAPTER 2

*There is nothing more exciting than being part of a local church
and seeing that church reach new levels in the glory of God.*
—Terry Nance

Dad had many church stories and was very fond of his
heritage in the black church of the Deep South. He loved to
talk about the special experiences he had at the Macedonia
Baptist Church in Opelika, Alabama. He often reflected on
the old folk of the town and how they held a unique
relationship with each other, in particular, as Christians. They
often boasted of their white-framed, one-roomed Negro
church and the powerful sermons preached by the itinerate
pastor who went from one church to another on horse and
buggy. In the South, they had too few preachers to pastor
churches and many ministers would preach at a church twice
a month and on the fifth Sunday. The deacons and trustees
were in charge of worship the other Sundays and were placed
in a very authoritative position. They held the church together

until the preacher could come by on his respective Sunday.

My father often told porch stories about his pastor, the Rev. Jordan of Macedonia Baptist Church. He would say he could preach the beard off a billy goat. One day while we all assembled on the porch, he told us about the death of Rev. Jordon. Dad said, "We had church in those days! The little church might have been small but it was filled with the Holy Ghost. You could feel the presence of God even at a distance before you would get to the building. I shall never forget one day that my granddad, and me, I called him Pa Pa, would go to open the church for late night service. He was the janitor of the church and I was a little boy. PaPa said to me, 'LJ, let's go and open the doors of the church for the revival service tonight.' It was late fall and the sun went down early and it would get real dark in the South. We had to come through the woods, briars, and trees. Those trees would sway at night as if they were alive. We would have to come through the woods almost all the time. I was usually afraid, not of the deep darkness because PaPa always had a lantern at night, but I was afraid of the snakes. Yes, children in the South knew snakes were always around and reminded us of the serpent Satan. But PaPa was never afraid of snakes.

"That evening we were headed up the hill, through the woods, with the lantern lit, to open the doors of the church and warm the church up. On this one particular evening, we were walking up the hill, and quite a distance before we reached the building, you would never believe what we saw.

We were looking up the hill at the church and sure enough, the church house was lit. Pa said to me, 'Well, I guess someone got there ahead of us and turned on the lights.' When we got a little closer, we could hear the music and the choir just a-singing. I could hear the loud expressions of gratitude and the people yelling 'Amen' and 'Thank You, Jesus.' It appeared as if, not only that church had started, but that the people were having a good time. When we got closer we could see shadows of people dancing and shouting in the spirit. Yes, they were having a good time. The only thing we noticed was that there were no cars on the outside and we thought everybody must have walked to the church. The closer we got to the church, the louder the people were. As we approached the door to go in, the moment we grabbed the door handle and turned it, everything got dark. We went inside and there was not a person in sight. PaPa went on as if nothing unusual had happened, and proceeded to turn on the lights and start the fire. I said, 'Didn't you hear all the sounds and notice the church was already lit?' He said, 'Yes, but sometimes the spirit of the church has to meet you before the Spirit in the church will come. And those were the spirits preparing us for the Spirit.' We both laughed and later on the real people showed up, even Rev. Jordan."

Dad often told us about how powerful a preacher the Rev. Jordan was, with his short, dark-skinned face and he always, wore a black suit, white shirt, a black tie, and black shoes. Of course, Dad probably never realized that these were the same clothes Rev. Jordan wore all the time because he didn't have any other Sunday-go-to-meeting attire. The town Dad grew up in was very poor. Dad would often tell us about how Rev. Jordan would preach so well until there was never a dry-eyed person in the church and everybody got happy. Later on, when I was grown, I met Rev. Jordan and heard him preach at a church service; he preached one of the worst sermons I had ever heard in my life. In fact, he was downright awful with all of his hollering with no context and even Dad had to admit this truth. Dad said maybe he thought those sermons were so good because he was too ignorant, himself, to know the difference.

My father often told us on the porch about Rev. Jordan's first death. That's right, Rev. Jordan died twice. Dad said, "On the day Rev. Jordan died, the entire town was in bereavement. Rev. Jordan was the only preacher we knew and he held the church together. On the day of his funeral flowers were everywhere. I can still smell those flowers today. And you couldn't get inside of the church for the press of the people. Whew, there were people from everywhere just to see the dead body of Rev. Jordan. He was lying down in that casket with his same old black suit, white shirt, black tie, and black shoes. Well, you know they didn't embalm in those days. They would lay your body out on a board called the 'cooling board' and let your warm body chill into death. The old mothers of the community would watch you all night long and that's what they call today a wake service. People who watched your body would stay awake all night to make sure the cats in the neighborhood didn't come by and mess up the body. Well, they watched Rev. Jordan's body all night while the men went out to dig the grave in the graveyard. The next day we would have the funeral.

"People were everywhere and it was hot in the church and the folk were just a-crying, but the choir started singing and somebody started one of those old Dr. Watts hymns, *I love the Lord, He heard my cry; and pitied every groan, long as I live where trouble rise; I'll haste unto His throne,* and folk just couldn't take it. They were just a-moaning and suddenly, right there in the casket, Rev. Jordan opened his eyes and started preaching! I remember his sermon. He sat up, opened his eyes, looked around and said, 'I died once and I ain't going to die no more.' He got out of the casket and went on to preach; people fell out like they never did before. Now, I know you children don't believe this story but I was there and I saw it with my own two eyes as a little kid. Of course, later on he did die, I am sure, but back then I think what happened, he was really not dead but unconscious. You know a lot of black people back then before they enbalmed people, were buried alive." Dad would then say, "Well, children, time to go to bed." Off we went after hearing about Rev. Jordan, the pastor who died twice, and the old people in the lit church.

Life Lessons You Can Take Away From this Story

Life is filled with strange experiences that we do not understand and there is an unseen world of spirits that do exist. When one dies and one's soul is separated from one's body, the entire essence of which that person was remains behind. This essence remains as long as memory remains of the loved ones who have passed on before us!

If the essence of the person does exist, then the remnants of their activities must remain in a real sense. In the lit-up church, there is an example of the real yet unreal; the fiery church that remains, as an example of what worship in the Christian experience ought to be like. However, when we enter into their seemingly unreal world as fleshly humans, we will be sure to see that all lights are turned off until we join their church experience in the world beyond.

GOD'S RIGHT EYE
He Sees All We Do

CHAPTER 3

God's eye is on the sparrow and I know He watches over me!
—Negro Spiritual

One night, Dad took all of us children outside on the big white front porch. Dad and Mom's house was a beautiful large brick home framed in white. My mother always wanted things matching in color. Mom didn't know you don't paint a front porch white, with a mechanic as a husband who usually came in covered with automobile oil, and nine messy children. That is the last thing a mother of fifteen knows. Oh, yes, Mom always took in at least six of our friends who claimed her as their other mother, especially at meal times. There was usually Derrick, whose mother was raising three of them without a husband, and Shorty, who was short, of course, and who tried to compensate for his size with long hair and usually wore a trench coat even in the summer; Julius, who lived up above the local bar as an only child with his mother, who held weekday parties, and Mike, our nephew. Then there was Becky, the next-door neighbor whose family was almost as large as ours. Anyway, my mom and dad entertained what sometimes seemed to be the whole neighborhood. After all, it was a community where everybody was somebody and somebody always knew the Macons. One would have thought with all that traffic, Mom would have chosen another color like black for her porch to save her from all the extra work of repainting the porch every four or five months.

It was on that porch that Dad would tell us about God's eyeball peeping through the night sky. Those of us who could, and were the oldest, usually got a seat in the chair while the rest of us would have to find seats on the steps or floor of the porch. There was usually a center chair that was larger than the rest and bounced a little. Dad would sit there and all of us, after having that same old plate of beans, fatback, and cornbread, would rush to the front porch and wait until the sun would go down. Of course, Dad would never let us sit in silence. He would bring some marbles and shoot marbles with us, or he would let us play hide-and-seek and, on occasion, he would be the counter facing the tree to find us little ones.

Soon, the day sky gave way to the veil of night, and darkness soon occurred. Of course, we would always have additions to his audience by evening, because it was always Dad and Mom's rule that everyone had to at least be on the porch when the streetlights came on. We were always told we didn't have to be in the house, but at least on the porch. And by the ruling of our parents, like in a baseball game with the runner barely touching the plate, we would be called "safe" if we made it on the porch by streetlight time.

I remember those days so well, when I rushed to make it to the porch right before the streetlights came on and Mother would be standing with her switch in hand. Oh! I forgot to tell you, Mom believed in every night priding herself in reaching for a very effective branch from the nearby tree, clearing it of thorns, and taking off the old bark to highlight and expose the glistening of the inner green. Of course, after many years, I really think she was making sure we learned the lesson before the experience of an old time spanking, that if one is playing on the outside there would be a mental image of the light green switch that appeared in our minds to remind us "Don't be late or you've got a date with the switch." Usually, I was never late.

But on this one occasion, I played ball too much or was having too much fun getting dirty, and it was about that time. I looked at the evening sky and all the signs were there, it was almost time and getting late. I started my run up Sycamore Hill, the largest hill in Cincinnati, around the curve to Bodman, up the hill, and lo and behold, like an Olympic runner humping for the last round, I started running, breathlessly looking toward the goal line and the encourager on the porch (the switch), and all the people. I started coming around the last lap. Mom on the porch, Dad in the big chair, my siblings shouting for victory, and lo and behold, I made it! All congratulated me and Mom, with her piercing eyes, hopeful that I would win and yet gleeful that she did not have to show the worst side of herself just before Dad's porch stories!

We all sat down; Dad cleared his throat, deepened his voice, swung back in his big chair and began to tell his stories. He proceeded to tell us about the night sky. "See those clouds, y'all?" We said, "Yes, Dad, I see them." But you always had the one who needed clarification, which was I. "Dad, do you mean the big one or the little ones?" Dad would say, "Son, just watch those clouds." And then he would say, "Beyond those clouds are the deep dark blue skies. And beyond the darkness are many and many universes, planets, and balls of fire." But then he would not stop there. He would inform us that "way beyond all of that are little lights." We would say, "Dad, we see them and they are so shiny and bright." Dad would then go into a theological discussion about what the lights were. What amazed me, and still does today, was that Dad often boasted about how he did not even have a third grade education and, yet, he understood the makeup of the constellations. He, in a proud, boastful voice, would say, "Children, beyond all those constellations are God's eyeballs! He's peeping down at everything and us. Look at all those stars and white holes. If that's His eyeball, just think about how big His body is. He's out there peeping at us and watching what each of you are doing. But not only is He peeping, He also wants you to know that He sees all your good works and all your bad works. So you have to be good in school. You have to be honest in your dealings with your friends, family, church, and teachers. You have to live a good life, 'cause God's big eye is watching. But know also that He's protecting us."

After telling his story of God's eye peeping through the sky, it would be time to go to bed. After all, we were some little ones. Before we would run into the house, Dad would always stop us with one more slant of the porch story. Here, he added, "Oh yes! I forgot to tell you that the light beyond the skies was not God's two eyes, but rather it was only His right eye, only *one* of them! Remember, He's a big God!" We rushed off to bed and after changing clothes, slept restfully, knowing that God's big right eye was protecting us, caring for us, and looking at us.

LIFE LESSONS YOU CAN TAKE AWAY FROM THIS STORY

One of the spirituals of the slaves was titled *His Eye Is on the Sparrow and I Know He Watches Over Me.* Their very existence relied on the all-seeing eye of God. The African of old had a saying, "God has big eyes and sees all we do."

The lesson we must learn from the porch story, *God's Right Eye,* is to have total dependence on an all-seeing Creator Who sees with both His left and right eye. The late Dr. Calvin Perkins related this total dependence upon God when he told of his experience as a student at Natchez College. He was down to one nickel in the early 1900s. It was a cold, icy day. About one half hour before the campus eatery closed, he went and purchased a nickel's worth of cheese and crackers. This was in the days when such items could be purchased for a nickel. On his way back to the dormitory, he slipped and fell on the ice. His cheese and crackers were smashed into crumbs, and scattered over the icy concrete walk. He hungrily climbed the stairs to his room that overlooked the icy spot. From his window he saw a crew of birds having a literal feast. They were eating and strutting with no thought of slipping on the ice. Dr. Perkins reported that when he saw their sole dependence upon their Creator, he learned to live by that secret, knowing that God, too, watches him. Therefore, he found that in the storehouse of God, within eyeshot, there is more care in God's economy than a nickel's worth of cheese and crackers. We, too, need to learn the secret that God's eyes are upon us at all times and that He cares for us!

PART TWO

STORIES THAT TEACH

─────── STORIES THAT TEACH ───────

THERE IS A saying, "Like father, like son" which is to suggest that the son learns from his father and transports those things taught by his father. Fathers exercise the greatest influences on our self-perceptions because we are the extension of their dreams, values, and prejudices. A father usually expects his children to become more than he became and accomplish more than he achieved.

As a father to my own two sons I continued this tradition of porch stories by using the porch and being as creative to them as my father was to me. I wanted to teach my sons that they could do anything they want to do. But in some ways, I wanted to guard them against pitfalls that can endanger a family or a group of young males, in particular African-American males, in today's society.

As their father, I taught them never to give in to the weaknesses of society and culture. I taught them that a strong mind would lead to a strong destiny. Where did I learn this? I discovered much of this from "The Teacher," my own father, who made me believe that the average person can rise above difficult circumstances even with limited resources and get the good work of God done.

FOLLOW THE MOON
Aim for High Goals

CHAPTER 4

In the long run, men hit only what they aim at. Therefore, they had better aim at something high.

—Henry David Thoreau

Though the South had its moments of challenge, Dad would tell us some of the joys of living in the South; the kindness of the blacks in the South, the silence of the night one could experience while sitting on the porch and listening to the outdoor country nightlife. Dad would often tell us how you hear the crickets and the movement of birds. He was well attuned to the natural environment of the earth. He often told us how fascinated he was with the sun, moon, and stars. In fact, one of his porch stories had to do with the moon.

On the evening of telling us the story "Follow the Moon," the moon was so bright it appeared as a hot ball of fire and was so close we could almost touch it. We had all settled down on the porch waiting for Dad to tell us the next porch story. This night Dad sat there like an astronomer as if studying the night sky. He sat there like a highly trained scholar with his head upward as if he knew astronomy. He acted like he had studied the nature of the universe including the sun, moon, planets, and stars. To us, he looked like a young Galileo or Albert Einstein. To this day, I think Dad was one of the smartest men who lived, yet without opportunity due to being brought up in a world of racism and discrimination. His greatest aspiration was but a dream.

On this night, Dad had a sandwich and a cup of Kool Aid as he began to tell us the story.

Dad said to us on that night, "Children, y'all look at the moon. Do you see it? Well, I almost touched it. That's right, one night in the Deep South, this same moon was up; and you know in the South, you could see the moon much brighter because it was so much darker. In the South you could cut the darkness with a knife. The moon was setting like this, and me and my friend, Black Jack, was sitting out in a field talking about our disdain for the white man. We had it hard in the South, where the very soul of the black man wasn't worth much and his intelligence wasn't valued any. (Dad could use those big words and we never could figure out where he got them.)

"My other friend, Big Jack and I looked up and lo and behold the moon was so bright and so big and so orange that we decided to touch it! We started off running towards it and we did run! We went through the fields and down the dirt road and up a hill and over a mountain, but the moon seemed to start running from us and so we chased it. At times, it started to move, and we moved with it, and where it went, we went with it. We were on a real chase but we had made up our minds that we were going to capture that moon. I will never forget that night. Big Jack could run for a fat boy and being thin and skinny, I knew I could run. But Big Jack just couldn't keep up with me! We ran and ran, hopped over bushes, ran through streams, jumped through back yards and the moon never would stop. We even saw it starting to go down and we tried to go down with it until soon it just disappeared behind a mountain. We were tired and just laid down in another field and concluded that we couldn't touch it that night. But we rested securely in knowing that this was the moon and after all, it would come up another night and we'd make another run for it then. Do you know what the moral and meaning of that story is children?

"It is this: There are some things in life you just will not be able to capture, and the moon is one of them! But just keep on chasing your dream and one day the moon will come up again and you might capture it. By the way, children, John Glenn went out in space today and he's up there trying to chase the moon. (That was the day he orbited the earth.) T.V. says that he's pretty close to it. Now, it is time to capture some sleep eye because I'm tired and had a hard day's work at the filling station, so I'm going to bed! See you in the morning." And off Dad went to rest, just to awaken and capture another successful day.

Life Lessons You Can Take Away From this Story

Dreams must always be pursued, even if it seems to be a pipe dream or a moon rush. We must forever pursue that which glows positively in front of us! There are times when we will pursue the dream through valleys, rivers, and mountain experiences in life. Also, there are times when pursuing the dream falls out of sight right before our eyes. We must never forget the words of Scarlett O'Hara, played by Vivien Leigh in the classic picture *Gone with the Wind.* When Rhett, played by the great actor Clark Gable, finally had enough of Scarlett's foolishness and disappointments, he affirmed his leaving their relationship as husband and wife. At the top of the staircase Scarlett pleads with Rhett to remain, to which Rhett says, "Scarlett, I ain't never coming back no more." Scarlett is fearful and begs for a change of heart on the part of Rhett and makes her energetic plea, to which Rhett responds, "I don't give a damn," and Scarlett allows him to leave with the final words of survival, affirming, "tomorrow is another day."

When one pursues the moon and finds total darkness, one must remember the words of Scarlett, "Tomorrow is another day," and so there must logically follow another night to which the moon shall return and the pursuit must continue.

THE GREAT TITANIC
The Survival of the Fittest

CHAPTER 5

A man just can't sit around and do nothing.
—Chip MacGregor

One of the most famous disasters in human history was when the great ship called *Titanic* sank in 1912. This ship was one of the greatest built in the twentieth century and was supposed to be unsinkable. The ship took its first, last, and only voyage and sank on April 15th of the same year. The ship, built with the latest technology of the day, was considered to be strong enough for any and all emergencies. People from all over the world came to see and board this great ship. There were people from countries such as Iran, France, and Italy. The captain of the ship was Edward Smith, a Jesuit who had served the great and rich J. P. Morgan. This powerful ship began its voyage from south England and was supposed to pass through the Atlantic Ocean. Captain Smith was known to be an excellent captain, having traveled the North Atlantic for over twenty-six years; he prided himself in knowing where every iceberg lay.

The journey of the *Titanic* was scheduled to begin in March 1912, but the construction of the ship could not be completed by then and coal fuel was not easily available at that time. The *Titanic* was registered in Liverpool and made its maiden voyage from Southampton. It was a cool, spring Wednesday morning. Many of the passengers from other ships were transferred to this "unsinkable" ship.

Some thought that no Negroes were on board and many blacks made fun of this unsinkable ship that sunk. My dad was one of them. Though he saw the sadness in the affair, he used his rich imagination and humor to display how blacks might have reacted had they been on the ship. Though I don't think my dad understood the entire story, he picked up on part of it and left us disappointed after not being able to complete the story. We all waited on the front porch to hear Dad's story of the great *Titanic* told over and over again, but never finished, leaving us to draw our own conclusions.

Dad would say, "Well, children, it was the twenty-fifth of May, that was a heck of a day, when the great *Titanic* sailed away. It was a luxury liner with passengers of all kinds, who lived lavish lifestyles. All sorts of entertainment were on the ship; everyone on board was all taking a sip. The ship was equipped with four 400 kilowatt generators, everybody was drinking and doing what not. The passengers were given separate quarters and were able to use electric lamps and so many other modern conveniences. Many were experiencing the high level facilities. A variety of foods were up on the deck. There were indoor games and outdoor gymnasiums, not a person was there without his possessions. To protect them from the cold were blankets and stuff, but by them stood a barrel full of laughs. Though the people were now a thousand miles apart, there was no worry cause they all had a cup. The radios on this ship had ranges of four hundred miles. They didn't worry and they were filled with smiles. Old Shine, the Negro, was on board the ship; he snuck in at the bottom of this brand new ship.

"It was May twenty-fifth that the *Titanic* took her maiden voyage. The passengers were asleep; to awake early the next day. On the next day, old Captain Smith looked out his window and frowned with a smile. There was a huge white iceberg and the ship was at full speed, running twenty-two knots on a moonless night. Captain Smith tried his best to move to the right, but the old ship was going too fast with its might. While half of the ship overcame the iceberg, the other half crashed into the rock solid iceberg. Shine was on board as the ship slowly began to sink. Women were running from deck to deck and the men said, 'Shoot, what the heck.' There was old black Shine, the black brother who slipped and glided on the unsinkable ship like a rat slipping and gliding in and out of a hole.

"Everybody on the ship was running and moving from side to side, some with clothes on and others with just sweat in their eye. But old black Shine was cool, calm, and collected because Old Shine knew how to swim. Shine leaped off with one of the most beautiful sprouts and with hands spread out he dived like a bird. Old Shine started swimming! Shine looked back and lo and behold, one of the most beautiful women that he ever could behold, yelled out, 'Shine, Shine! Please save me. I'll give you all the kissing that you'd ever did see.' Shine said, 'Kissing is good, but kissing won't last. Shine's gonna save his own black hide' and Shine kept swimming. Shine looked back and there was Rockefeller; he had bills coming right out of his collar. He said, 'Shine, Shine! Please save me. I'll give you all the money you can ever see.' Shine looked back and thought about the dollars and said to himself, 'Money is good, but money don't last. Shine gonna save his own black hide' and Shine kept on a-swimming. Well, the story is told that Shine kept on swimming, till somewhere around 2:20 in the morning, Shine looked back, the ship was on fire, the passengers started to holler, and the captain bid all farewell. Shine said to himself, 'The *Titanic* is good but the *Titanic* won't last, Shine is gonna save his own black hide.'"

Strangely enough, every time Dad told us the story of the great Titanic, the details and characters were altered. Sometimes the date of the disaster was May 25, even though it was not the day of the sinking. Often, I asked Dad whether he was sure it was the twenty-fifth day of May, because my history book would affirm it as being the 15th of April. He would lift his head high, close his eyes, pause with a long moment of thought and respond, "Shine was good and Shine did last. Shine says it was on the twenty-fifth of May that he saved his own black hide." Thus concludes the great day the *Titanic* sank, or at least how my father understood it.

LIFE LESSONS YOU CAN TAKE AWAY FROM THIS STORY

The sinking of the great *Titanic* was one of history's most tragic events and for those who survived, one of life's greatest victories. It is said that underneath the ship was printed the words "The Unsinkable." We know that all of life has its sinkable moments. Yet, the story tells us that with fortitude, strength, and the everlasting pursuit of life, one can continue to swim in life's ocean filled with problems. Though the waters of life may be chilly and cold and death may seem inevitable, one can pursue a course of action to survive in the most uncharted areas of life, even when self-survival becomes one's only reason for survival. Shine must save his own black hide for the sake of personal survival.

AIN'T GOING BACK NO MORE
The Problem of the South

CHAPTER 6

Today's mighty oak was yesterday's nut that held its ground.
— Unknown

That night, we waited on the porch for Dad to tell us one of his porch stories. This night he seemed a little sad because his eyes were drooping and he appeared to be a little tired. Deep within his consciousness, we knew something was going on. He worked for the white man in the 1960's and they were not always fair. Even though he owned a thriving automobile repair shop and gasoline station, he knew something strange was going on. He noticed that whites would come by and purchase gas and repair their cars at the gas station as long as they knew he was the worker and not the owner. But when the white owner sold the business to him, a Negro, the white customers stopped coming and things were hard. Years later, after Martin Luther King, the Atlanta preacher, died and right after Dad sold his station to a white man because whites would not patronize his business, this gas station became one of the most thriving businesses in Cincinnati, Ohio. I guess, as the old saying goes, *the white man's ice is a bit cooler than the Negro's.*

Anyhow, Dad came in a little tired and worried but he never wanted us children to know. But we knew something was wrong when he came home. After whistling a tune before he entered the house to let us kids know of his arrival, he came into the house. Then he hugged us all as we yelled, "Daddy's home" and he went to wash up, change clothes, and sit next to the stove with his hands warming in an open oven. But suddenly he sat with a hand-in-cheek position, as if to say, "What am I going to do next?" After satisfying his cold hands that had been used to repair cars at another dealer all day, on a cool evening he summoned all of his children to the porch. Of course, Mama said, "Put your sweaters on cause it's cool outside and I don't want no one to catch cold cause if you do, you have to take a dose of Father John or castor oil." Most of us knew what Father John was and didn't want it, and we definitely did not want castor oil. Father John was that chocolate light brown stuff in a brown bottle with a picture of Father John on the label that looked like an early eighteenth century monk that tasted good until you got a spoon full. Castor oil was that thick, nasty tasting clear liquid that went down your throat like an ocean full of seaweeds. It was just plain awful!

When we got to the porch, Dad seemed to be better now! He'd warmed up while his family had rushed to the porch.

He was sitting in his seat of authority, and on the front porch of the house he was now in his neighborhood, where he boasted life was more like a brotherhood. He said to us kids, "I want to tell you a story about my early upbringing and why I left the South."

"I grew up in the Deep South of Alabama in a city called Opelika." It wasn't until we got grown that we realized Daddy didn't really know the name of the place he really grew up at because he was always moving from house to house during the late fall of each year. You see, my daddy was raised on a sharecropper farm. His daddy, our supposed grandfather, and maybe even uncle was a sharecropper for the white man. (My dad never could with assurance tell us who were the two old people who raised him. That's another porch story to be told.) Like many blacks in the 1930's, they would receive housing, which usually meant an old shack or barn, with a bed and a few old furnishings and an old mule they called Ole Charlie and some seed to plant in the spring. They would work the white man's farm in the South all year and somewhere in the late fall or even at Christmas time they would settle up. Few of his children knew that when settling up time came, that moment when the sharecroppers had to pay for borrowed product for planting, the white landowner also deducted the debt of the land usage fee for housing and other supplies the sharecropper had put on credit from the local store to sustain his family, in order to work the land throughout the year. Usually, at the end of the year the landowner would tell the black sharecropper, "You had a good year, you broke even." My dad said on the porch, every year his dad broke even and never profited from sharecropping so he, like many other blacks during those times, would load up their belongings and move to another land where the vicious cycle went on year after year on almost every land in the South. So Dad really didn't know where he was raised because there were so many sections around Opelika, Alabama. By the way, Dad always spelled the city Opeleka and never Opelika, maybe because he only wished he lived in the big city of Opelika, which was really a little town. To him it was better than saying, "I lived in an area so far back in the country that they had to pump light in that section of town and we never knew the name."

Dad said he never loved the South but liked all of his buddies. There was Jibber, who he thought was his cousin, though when I met him years ago there was no resemblance between this deep dark man and my very light complexioned and almost white looking father. He often boasted of Big John, who was an extremely large black man who looked something like the prizefighter, Jack Johnson, and a few other friends that Dad proudly called "true friends". Later on, Dad even told us how Big John would always fight for him when young boys in the neighborhood wanted to beat up the half Negro who looked more white than black and had girly looking hair because he had long jet-black hair and seldom could afford a haircut! But when big black John was around, not even the real Jack Johnson could out-box Dad's friend,

Big John!

Therefore, even though Dad did not like the racism and discrimination in the South, he liked his neighborhood friends who would take up for him. When he got old enough to drink, and that was before he was of legal age to drink, he would always remember those who were like a brother. But Dad, on this night, was going to tell us why he left the South and promised himself he was never going back. I am sure you think it was because of sharecropping, Ole Charlie the Mule, and moving from land to land. No, that was not quite it.

On this night, Dad would tell us! He told us about how he had made a visit to his home when he was a sergeant in the army. After joining the army and learning how to read, and at least, write his name, he decided to visit his parents while on leave from the service. He often talked about how proud his parents were of him because he was their only child, or at least, he thought so. But that's another porch story. Dad was ready to tell us why he left the South!

I remember that night because Dad seemed concerned and maybe even worried. When he sat in his chair, with eyes drooping, he said, "Now, when I was in the South, things were very rough. The white man didn't like the black man and to be frank with you children, I was never fond much of him either. He didn't always give us a fair shake and to be honest, I was tired of Ole Charlie the mule, the shacks, and moving every year. Well, on this occasion, I had just got home

69

from the army. Ma and Pa, that's what I use to call my granddad and grandma, but really I never knew what relation they were to me. I just remember they were the only mother and father I knew. They were really proud of me joining the army and serving my country even though they knew I was too young to be in the service. I came home to visit them to show them how I had grown up and to show off my uniform.

"One day, I decided to go down to the local store and get me a soda pop. It was really hot that day and I was real thirsty. I went to the store and sat down at one of their counters, and really us blacks had no right to sit at the white man's counter, we normally went to the back of the store and knocked on the door. But that day I went to the front and asked the store clerk to give me a Coke. And the store clerk thought I was getting smart with him because the custom was for Negroes to ask for a soda pop, not the specific name brand of the soda and the clerk would give them any kind the clerk wanted us to have, whether it was a Coke, Pepsi, or orange soda pop. The clerk looked me dead in the eye and told me, 'Nigger, get out of here. You trying to get smart in here!'

"Well, I had just served my nation in war and was now made conscious of a new world and so I was sick and tired of Ole Charlie, the mule, and how the white man treated my family as sharecroppers, and now this store clerk was added to my list and so I picked up the empty Coke bottle next to me and threw it upside his head after he called me a nigger. And boy, was I scared! I ran out of that store straight towards home. I told my mother and father what happened and they were so upset they made me a little lunch, a sandwich, and an apple and told me to rush to the nearest train and get out of town because they were sure I'd be dead by sundown. Of course, they didn't have to tell me that because I had already promised myself that I was leaving the South and was never coming back!

"My mother and father already knew the threat of the South on the life of a Negro man because when I was a youngster, one day I stole a little pig and brought him back home to eat. I remember, sitting on the porch earlier that day, like we are doing now, and it was a hot day, and my parents didn't have any food in the house. My dad only had one piece of bread and he served it to me, a twelve year old child, after putting some jelly between it and slicing it in half, one for me and the other half for himself. After we went out on the porch, my dad tried to comfort me by stretching his hands wide and patting proudly on his stomach, exclaiming how full he was. He said to me, 'LJ, I am so full I couldn't eat another thing and that was the best sandwich I've had in years.' Of course, I was still hungry and I never felt the fullness of a half slice of bread with jam in the center. I knew what I was going to do. I went down to one of the landowners' farms with a hammer in my hand. I peeped through some bushes and saw some pigs on the white man's farm. It was late at night and so, like an army soldier approaching the enemy camp, I crept up on one of those baby pigs and with one blow, hit him in the head and threw it over my shoulder. I came home and laid the pig on the supper table and told my dad, 'Now this will fill us up!' My dad just shook his head and Momma was so scared she just knew I'd be lynched before morning. Of course, what they did was, knowing that they, too, were hungry, and we couldn't return the dead pig to the owner, she pulled out the pots and pan, boiled some water, cooked the pig and we all ate the whole pig that night. It was so funny because my mother was more scared of the smell of pig frying in the pan than anything else. She knew the white man might smell that pig and find the culprit who stole it.

"My parents knew how bad the white man treated Negroes when they were not doing anything wrong, and how much worse they would be treated for stealing a pig, and so they were sure that I would be killed for hitting a white man upside of his head with a Coca-Cola bottle. I jumped a train and headed for Chicago but I never will forget that white man's eyes when I hit him. I felt so good because it was what I wanted to do to the white man for a long time. Not all whites were bad, but this one and those landowners were terrible people. And I promised myself from that moment on that I was leaving the South and ain't never going back no more. Well, boys and girls, it's nighttime and you know what that means. That's right, time to go to bed." And off we went after hearing why my Dad left the South and wasn't ever going back!

LIFE LESSONS YOU CAN TAKE AWAY FROM THIS STORY

Racism has been deeply embedded in our society and unfortunately, it has shown itself within the early and late twentieth century. Jim Crow reared its ugly head in American society like never before. There were many blacks who rejected the inequities of those injustices and defied their many forms of expression. Many blacks rejected segregation at the expense of losing their lives and leaving their families in the South during the great migration period of the 1920s. For them, they left the South of oppression for the North of liberation and freedom, only to discover that, as Martin Luther King, Jr., suggested, "Injustice anywhere is a threat to justice everywhere."

WHO'S MY BABY'S DADDY?
An Unwanted Pregnancy

CHAPTER 7

When my father and my mother forsake me, then the Lord will take care of me.

—Psalm 27:10

LJ Macon, that was his name at birth in Alabama. Of course, Dad didn't really know what LJ stood for in his name because in the early 1900s, blacks didn't get birth certificates and many only were given initials as names. Dad would often tell me of midwives. These were women who would come to your house during the time of delivery and were experts in delivering babies. They knew how to clear and clean the house out and prepare for one of the greatest events of humanity—childbearing. They usually came over with their aprons and had their hair covered with an old white scarf. The headscarf would match their long white dress and if you didn't know it, you would have thought they were trained nurses and doctors. Thank God for the midwives.

When Dad was born, there were no midwives, no doctors, and certainly no birth certificates because these were extremely poor Negroes, second-class citizens, and happenchance folk—they just happened to be here in America. They had no rights, no equality, and certainly no privilege to pursue the American dream. And even if you were like my dad, half-white and Indian mixed with black blood, you still didn't count. That was evident in his name— LJ. Someone didn't even have the decency to give him a legitimate name. For many years, we children thought his name was spelled Eljay, not L. J. We thought his name was kind of cool because it matched his tender face and jet-black hair and we thought he was called that because, like a jaybird and a black crow, Dad was slick. But not slick enough to slide by being born nameless and without a midwife.

But Dad was a survivor. He often talked about how he had more lives than a cat. He told us how he survived Ole Charlie the mule and the white landowners; he made it through World War II and even that Japanese man he tripped over and wasn't killed. That's right, Dad told us about one incident when he first went to war. One evening he was hanging out with the boys and forgot his weapon and was returning through the bushes only to come upon an armed Japanese soldier. He told us how when he tripped over the soldier, the man looked at him stunned and he looked at the man stunned and all he and the young Japanese soldier did was to take off in opposite directions. Dad even survived the war when some of his closest buddies didn't make it. But Dad was reluctant to talk about that. He would talk about surviving poverty in the city. He was a survivor. But he still didn't have a real name and no midwife. He's only called LJ Macon! I am sure you want to know what happened.

The story goes that when Dad was born his mother was only thirteen. This he knew, by mere calculation of the date of her birth and the year he was born, which meant his mother was only thirteen years older than he. Her name was Mary and to this day, she is referred to as Ms. Mary. Anyone can tell you that a thirteen-year-old girl having a baby is victimized by molestation; after all, it takes nine months for a full-term pregnancy. That means she may have been impregnated at the age of twelve. It was said that in those parts of Alabama, a young girl seldom would escape being raped by the white man, the black man, or the Indians. That's right. Later on, we discovered there was an Indian tribe that was forced from Florida to the Alabama shores. They were mean Indians and would take young girls in a minute and make them their own. It's said that an Indian raped Grandma Mary. After all, when looking at Dad you knew that he was part Indian with his high cheekbones, and part white with his light complexion and part black. Miss Mary never told my father who her baby's daddy really was. Also, he had no other siblings. It's said that after Dad was born, Miss Mary's baby was taken to the barn where some old folk found him and took him and nursed him as their own. Their names were

Lucinda, a short dark-looking black woman and Robert, a very light-complexioned black man. They became my dad's parents, Robert and Lucinda Macon.

Rumor has it that Robert Macon was dad's biological father, because he looked so much like my father. Then, if that were the case, he would be the culprit of the rape. Others, have called him Uncle Robert because he was in some way a distant kin to my father. However, my father just called him Pa Pa because he was the kindest old man he'd ever met. His wife, Ma Ma, was his best friend; a short black woman with nothing but purity in her eyes and voice. Dad often boasted about how God was gracious to him for keeping his biological mother away from him because he was raised with not only Southern hospitality but also Southern love. Dad loved these two old people.

One day, Dad felt a real urgency to take a leave from the army and head back home to Alabama. Unfortunately, it was said, a bad accident happened to the only mother and father he knew. When he arrived, the house had been burned down. It was said that PaPa was cooking and some of the grease accidentally spilled causing the house to catch on fire. But others rumored that it was an intentional fire. It was said that Robert Macon was the descendent of a rich landowner with the last name Macon who disowned his only biological son, Robert. It was rumored that Robert was due the inheritance owed him by this rich landowner and to prevent the inheritance from passing down the line, they killed Pa by way of the fire. Lucinda, also known as Ma, tried to get in the house to rescue the old man from the house fire. Unfortunately, the two of them made their exit to their eternal destination on the same night. Dad got there to Alabama, and only wanted one thing, the washbasin and pitcher and couldn't get that because it had already been stolen from the house. Years later, he said he saw it on the top of his cousin Jeter's kitchen refrigerator. To this day, Dad doesn't know who his father was and what his real name would have been and he had no midwife to birth him into this awful world.

So when Dad got to the army he made up a name after taking the initials L. J. to mean Louis James. But later, he discovered that in the South there were many others born with only initials for their names. He even met a friend in Cleveland, an old deacon of the Mt. Zion Church, named S.C. Jester who grew up in Georgia and had a midwife to birth him but no name, just S.C.

Dad knew how to fix anything and always used his favorite phrase, "If there's a will, there's a way." And he discovered how to fix his not having any midwife and no family. He went and met a girl named Delina and asked God to give him as many children as possible, preferably boys. He had nine children altogether, seven boys and two girls. And when his sister-in-law died, he gained five more, three boys and two girls. Though Dad had nobody when he was born, he ended up having more than a midwife when he left. He had a name, Louis James, and a host of family.

Life Lessons You Can Take Away
From this Story

We live in a time where the deterioration of the family has occurred for many generations and the abuse from one generation to another remains. Unfortunately, sexual abuse of children is an age-old problem that yet persists in our society. Many have either attempted to abort their child or abandon their responsibility. However, whether abortion or abandonment becomes one's choice, God ultimately has the final word in the affairs of humankind. Ultimately, the children's song of the black church prevails: "He's Got the Little Bitty Baby in His Hands." One must believe once turned over into the mighty hand of God, He will help in the pursuit of destiny which leads not only to the road of survival, but the ultimate end of success and reconciliation in one's life. "Who's my Baby's Daddy" when no daddy is around? It is God Who steps in as father by proxy, Who nurtures us through this unfriendly world.

THE DAY DADDY DIED
The Beginning of the End

| CHAPTER 8 |

When you pass through the waters, I will be with you, and through the floods, they shall not overflow you; when you pass through the fire, it shall not kindle upon thee, neither shalt thou be burned.

—Isaiah 43:2

It was a Tuesday morning, at about 5:30 a.m. that my father, Louis Macon, took his eternal flight to Heaven, a promotion and transition that will stay with me for a lifetime. Early that morning, I was awakened by a frantic call from my brother, Elmer, who said, "Larry, get up! Dad's house is on fire and I'm headed there now." I will never forget those words. The emergency lifeline called my house and told me that the house was on fire and that Dad and Walter were trapped inside.

I'm nearing the house now. "O my God, it's terrible, Preacher (That's what they called me.) and it looks real bad. I don't think anyone will make it out. O my God, Larry." There's

Robert (*my brother*). (*I was hearing Elmer talking to Robert,* 'How's Dad and Walt?'). Larry, it's real bad! Dad and Walt didn't make it out! They died! (*Elmer was talking again to Robert.*) "Daddy died in the fire, but Walter did not. Preacher, you better come down right now. It's real bad!" (*Phone hung up.*)

My family and I left our house that morning to see one of the most terrible tragedies in my life! Dad, the strong patriarch of a long line of children, had been killed in a devastating house fire.

That day, reporters wanted to hear my reaction and thoughts of this terrible accident. For the next day, a Cleveland Dealer newspaper reporter wanted to tell our story because they heard that my father had raised nine children of his own and five other children in this small frame house. The story was superb and was read all over the community. A picture of Dad with his drooping eyes and his favorite old cap was seen on every Metro section of the *Plain Dealer* paper. The article was titled, "Family Patriarch, 83, Killed in Cleveland Fire." If the story were retold on the porch it could read something like this:

Growing up without parents in Opelika, Alabama, a deep isolated Southern town, just an hour-and-half drive from the great city of Atlanta, Georgia, was a man named L.J. Macon who later changed his name to Louis James Macon. However, many called him Lou. Young LJ or Lou, as he was called, swore he would one day have a large, upstanding family whether it was in the South or North. L.J. died on a Tuesday, just a week after having his annual Fourth of July celebration, where he usually was the head chef and cook for the family in the backyard. That's right, every Fourth of July, Dad would get up at about 3 a.m., in the dark, go to the garage, and pull out his favorite barbeque pits that he had made to beat any and every one of his kids in making ribs, chicken, and hot dogs. For over sixty years he would win the "family rib burn off" contests. This year was no different. He won and all nine of his children lost!

It was that Tuesday after the Fourth of July week, the year 2005; Dad's dream of having a large family was finally accomplished! He reached the grand old age of eighty-three, with nine grown children, five adopted children, and more than sixty grandchildren and great-grandchildren.

His extended family was larger still. He was the patriarch of the community. Everybody knew Mr. Louis Macon because he would hang out with the boys in the neighborhood and as he sat on his front porch on East 116th or at the side of the house, which was really his driveway, he'd always wave at the folk in the community. Dad was a hit with everybody and never feared anybody.

Of course, he'd always talk about taking his daily ride to the park, or eating down at Old Joe's Restaurant in Cleveland and never leaving the house without his personal trusted companion, his dog, Spot, his Bible, and naturally, his Smith & Wesson. That's right, Dad always carried a pistol. He had a license for it and one day, Dad explained why he carried a gun. Dad said he always felt like one day he'd see his car driving away from the house and he would have to shoot the car to stop it. We'd ask him if he would be shooting at the driver of the car. Dad would reply, "Oh, no. I would never shoot or harm anybody, just the car. I would afterward say to the police who would be taking down the report, 'Sir, if you thought that I was shooting at the driver who was stealing my car, I was not! I was only shooting at my car because my car has no business going down the street without me inside.'" Of course, Dad would laugh every time after telling this story and we'd always laugh tears of amazement whenever he would tell us how he would handle a stolen car.

Dad was also a Christian man. That's right, he loved his church and served as a deacon at Mt. Zion Church of Oakwood Village, where his son, the Rev. Dr. Larry L. Macon, Sr. was pastor. He'd enjoy the choir and would declare there was never a bad sermon preached by his son. Of course, he did have a critical mind and would sometimes say to his son, "Son, you almost had it today to lift my spirit, but you didn't quite make it. You stepped on the grapes but didn't quite break them. You just stepped on them. So next Sunday, break the grapes!" Usually, that meant you did better than the average preacher in town but you could have done better. Most times, he was right!

L.J. was born in 1922. As a young man, he left his small hometown in Alabama to work as a truck driver. Lou, as he was sometimes called, married Delina after getting her father's permission. That's right, all of mamma's sisters and brothers had to receive their father's permission to get married. Granddad Elmer approved all but one. Elmer didn't like him because he thought this one was just too smart for his breeches. Years down the road, Granddad learned to appreciate the one son-in-law he didn't really like. Of course, Dad was his best son-in-law! Gramps liked LJ because LJ was like him; LJ cared less whether he gave permission to release his daughter or not. She'd be released one way or the other, voluntarily or involuntarily, Dad later told us!

Dad was a very proud man. The family could have qualified for public assistance, but they never applied. Dad would work day and night to provide for his family. Dad settled his family in Cincinnati, where he was one of the first Negroes to own a gas station in an all-white area. That was before King and his dream in Washington ever occurred. He was so proud he refused to have any of his children on any county assistance program, and made sure that the jails didn't pay for the upkeep of any of his boys. He believed in family discipline and often told us, when we were grown, about his strategy of getting the truth out of the one child he knew would always speak up when information on the others were needed. That was Walter, second oldest brother. Dad would demand certain information while my older brothers would always vow some kind of secret fraternity-ship. Dad would then take off his belt quickly, raise it up, and say, "I'll get the truth out of all of you." Then he would proceed to the bathroom where he'd turn on the bath water. But the water was not to bathe in but to take the time to soak his belt. We'd all hear the water running and pray that the culprit would come forth with words of wisdom, explained in humility, and baptized with much truth.

To our surprise, the older brotherhood was seldom that smart. Dad would then line the older brothers at the bed, making them kneel in a praying position and place them in a certain order, with the ones he thought were hard-core first, deceivers second, and then the brother who couldn't stand much pain. Dad would start with Rick, the oldest brother, bring out the wet belt he'd soaked in the bathtub, raise it up high in the air, and like a cowboy getting ready to lasso a young calf, he whirled it around a couple of times in the air, raised it high as if it had just become heaven bound and then lower it as if it had just descended from Heaven to the drudgery of hell, and then "Pow," it would hit the first boy who would scream awful. The second child in the line up was usually Walt. Dad always knew that once he gave the first child a lick of the belt, the second one, if it was Walt, would always give fully detailed information on any and all mischief of the day. Walt had a usual pattern of confession. He would always wait until the others were disciplined and then he'd jump off his knees and yell, "Dad, I'll tell you who it was that committed the crime and tell you all you wish to know, just don't whip me." And sure enough, Dad's truth serum usually worked and it kept all of us out of jail!

Well, Dad died Tuesday in a house fire. Mom always told him never to smoke in bed and usually Dad did what Mom said until Mom went to glory in 2002. Dad had been sick for several months before the accident, being in and out of hospitals and nursing homes, having had several surgeries to which he almost lost his life. On that dreadful day, being restricted to a wheelchair and having the difficulty of moving freely and walking, he emerged early in the morning to get relief from that last smoke of a cigarette, we think, and no doubt accidentally dropped it, and Dad was transported to Heaven!

Hopefully, the reader can finish the story in his and her own life when the last minute of this life is over, and ask what will be their story of the day after this life? *For we know that if our earthly house of this tabernacle were dissolved, we have a building of God, a house not made with hands, eternal in the heavens* (II Corinthians 5:1, KJV).

In the *Moody Monthly*, published in 1952, these words gave my heart contentment:

> **Five Minutes After . . .**
> It may be a moment, or after months of waiting, but soon I shall stand before my Lord. Then in an instant all things will appear in a new perspective.
>
> Suddenly the things I thought important—tomorrow's tasks, the plans for the dinner at my church, my success

or failure in pleasing those around me—these will matter not at all. And the things to which I gave but little thought—the word about Christ to the man next door, the moment (how short it was) of earnest prayer for the Lord's work in far-off lands, the confessing and forsaking of that secret sin—will stand as real and enduring.

Five minutes after I'm in Heaven I'll be overwhelmed by the truths I've known but somehow never grasped. I'll realize then that it's what I am in Christ that comes first with God, and that when I am right with Him, I do the things which please Him.

I'll sense that it was not just how much I gave that mattered, but how I gave it—and how much I withheld.

In Heaven I'll wish with all my heart that I could reclaim a thousandth part of the time I've let slip through my fingers, that I could call back those countless conversations which could have glorified my Lord—but didn't.

Five minutes after I'm in Heaven, I believe I'll wish with all my heart that I had risen more faithfully to read the Word of God and wait on Him in prayer— that I might have known Him while still on earth as

He wanted me to know Him.

A thousand thoughts will press upon me, and though overwhelmed by the grace that admits me to my heavenly home, I'll wonder at my aimless earthly life. I'll wish . . . if one may wish in Heaven—but it will be too late.

Heaven is real and hell is real, and eternity is but a breath away. Soon we shall be in the presence of the Lord we claim we serve. Why should we live as though salvation were a dream—as though we did not know?

"To him that knoweth to do good, and doeth it not, to him it is sin."

There may yet be a little time. A new year dawns before us. God help us to live now in the light of a real tomorrow!

I have to this day never feared my Dad's death nor the kind of death he died because I am sure in less than five minutes, Dad was in Heaven. *We are confident, I say, and willing rather to be absent from the body, and to be present with the Lord* (II Corinthians 5:8 KJV). I preached my Dad's eulogy one week later.

Some Through the Waters; Some Through the Fire!
Isaiah 43:2

These are strange and confusing moments. Death is a mystery and the death of our father, your grandfather, Uncle J as some called him lived a good life. He lived more than eighty-three years. He would always remind us that God only promises us three score and ten, but if by reason of strength they be four score...which means anyone given more than seventy years is on bonus years. God gave our father some thirteen bonus years.

And as Elmer, my younger brother stated to the media regarding this tragedy, "We really did not want him to go out like that!" We would have preferred that he die of old age in a natural death where vital signs just shut down. He was there at Marymount Hospital, stayed in Cleveland Clinic and we visited too numerous times at Parma General Hospital. He stayed several times at Rehab Centers. And if the truth were told we would rather him to have died there. But, in reality, if the truth was told, we would rather him never to have died, and especially not by way of a house fire.

We believed that Dad was a good man. Not perfect, but good and decent, and like all of us, he made his mistakes. The Bible does remind us "All have sinned and fallen short of the glory of God." No, he was not without sin, without flaws, without issues, but basically and intrinsically, he was a moral

90

man. His character was good. He was raised in the South with that southern mannerism of being hospitable and decent. He was raised in the South in 1922, some 200 miles outside of Birmingham. But, not really. He was born in a place called Opelika. But, not really. He was born in one of the areas near Opelika. But not really. Actually, he was born in a barn and we do not know where that was located so he just said he was born in Opelika.

Louis J. Macon was raised in a time when America's moral values were not so good. It was a time when racism and Jim Crow Laws in effect discriminated against the rights of a black man. He was from a poor family with no opportunities for survival. He often told us how he was the son of a sharecropper and each year they had to move from one farm to another because the owner of the field never gave justice to the worker of the land.

Dad often told us how segregation by whites was not always their main problem. But because Indians were forced from their reservations in north Florida and pushed to the Alabama area, they were sometimes angry at this injustice. Many lived on reservations in Alabama and expressed their anger in the form of abuse towards blacks. He informed us how he was told that his mother, at the young, tender age of thirteen was raped by Indians, or perhaps it was some white man, or even his own relative. He did not quite know who his father was but he does remember how he was later informed that when he was born his mother was so confused about it and refused to share her pregnancy with her own mother. She went to a barn and self delivered the baby and left him in the barn to die. But daddy survived because he said, he always remembered that saying, "God takes care of fools and babies." He believed that God never quite leaves infants and children in barns to die. A man and his wife, named Robert and Lucinda Macon, took him and raised him as their own. Our family does not quite know who these people were in relation to our father. Sometimes he said that it was his uncle, other times he thought that these were his grandparents. Finally, he would just say, "They were two angels sent from above." He would affirm, "Yes, they were angels of mercy" and so he just called them "MaMa" and "PaPa". I keep telling you who are adopted parents and stepparents to stop worrying about what your stepchildren and adopted children are calling you. If you be good to them, angel-like to them, they will soon drop the "step" and "adopted" and just call you Mom and Dad.

They called my dad "LJ". Back then, initials were used for slaves to dehumanize them and help them lose their identity. I heard of a former slave called "Iona" and her mother called her that to really mean "I Own Her" and she refused to take on one of those master's names. She didn't quite know her family's African tribal name.

But what Dad remembers most are those times in church and those moments with his family. Since he was an only child he asked God early in life to give him a large family with a majority boys. God blessed him and my mother with seven boys and two daughters. Then when my father's brother-in-law killed my mother's sister in Las Vegas, they adopted five more—three boys and two girls. When my mother's family held a family meeting to decide on which extended family member would raise one or two of the children, it was my dad who said, "If you can't take them all, take none at all because a family needs to be raised together." He raised not only his nine, but also an additional five all who were about the same age.

I don't know how Dad did it but he raised the fourteen of us. He worked hard while mother assisted in their family traditions. Every night Dad would come home tired and warm his hands in the open oven, eat dinner and then take us all out on the front porch and tell us his "Porch Stories." These were inspiring, exciting and uplifting moments.

After telling his stories and sending us to bed, he'd stay up late at night talking to the love of his life, Delina Macon. She was an extremely beautiful woman in looks and character. She often bragged about how she had never taken a drink in her life. She believed in moral values and raising her children and making sure they had clean clothes for school and three meals a day. Dad often told us about how he met her in Hazard, Kentucky, and married her two weeks later and ten years later had nine kids. But that's enough about this marvelous man's life.

Let me tell you about his death. He died in a fire. He's highly medicated taking eight pills per day. He has a hip replacement and usually never smokes in bed. He gets up at 4:30 a.m., and must have been somewhat delirious and probably thinks he's in the living room where he would get up and take a cigarette smoke. He never smoked in the bedroom and was often told by our mother not to do so. He is immobilized by a wheel chair. He lights a match that catches the bed on fire and the rest is history.

I started this sermon by saying this is a confusing moment for us. But there are "Confusing Moments in Life." We are here at this funeral service, confused. Death by fire, confused. But I will never forget that confusing moment when I first heard that the house was on fire. I went over that moment just a few days ago, after the house burning and Dad's death, and I kept replaying the accident in my mind. I will never forget these past days of sleepless nights. But it was this past Monday morning when God spoke to me. For some strange reason, I could not sleep all night. But somehow, I kind of dozed off during the early morning. About 4:30 a.m. I woke up and was watching a 1920 classic movie, for about seven minutes, that's somewhere between 4:30 a.m. and 4:37 a.m. I was looking at this classic movie from the 1920's. My dad was born in the 1920's and somehow if you live right, God will keep you connected with your parents. He'll wake you up early in the morning and make you watch a movie to remind you of your loved one's moments in life.

Somehow, I dozed back off and was awakened at 5:15 a.m., about the same time I got the news that my father's house was on fire. I saw a fireman who was talking on the news about how he saved someone in the September 11, 2001 Twin Towers tragedy. The news commentator asked the question, "Did he make it?" and the answer was "Yes." I heard Heaven kicking within my spirit. The question that remained in my mind was what happened to my father? Did he make it? Did he get through this tragedy? Was he in Heaven before all of the destruction of the fire damaged him? And the answer came to me that while earth was acting, in a raging fire, Heaven was responding in an awesome way: "To be absent from the body is to be present with the Lord" and "When this old earthly tabernacle is dissolved, I have another building not made with hands." But the real text that came to me, that gave me relief to my questions was this: Isaiah 43:2 says: "When thou walkest through the fire, thou shalt not be burned." Isaiah 49:16 says: "Behold, I have graven thee upon the palms of my hands, thy walls are continually before me." The Bible says, "Some through the water and some through the fire. But I have graven you in the palm of my hand."

PART THREE

ALWAYS IN CONTROL

ALWAYS IN CONTROL

OUR CHILDHOOD AND youthful experiences help us cut the psychological umbilical cord that causes us to become independent and seek our own levels of control. On many occasions, I have faltered because of my own need to be controlling, and I thank God that both family and friends overlook my faults because they were aware that growth in humans is a process.

I learned that I enjoyed doing things with living organisms even if they are as small and miniscule as ants. I learned that an adventurous life could be healthy when even learning and understanding the need for one's own sense of control. I am thankful for parents who've allowed me to be wrong in times when I felt the need to be in control, yet loved me enough to tell me when I was wrong and allowed me to return to the family after wronging others and being wrong. Through nature and sometimes my friends, they taught me to be a person who even my mother could not control. I am grateful that I saw my "transgressions" through their eyes. Sometimes my friends controlled me; at other times, I walked away to become the person in control and to become my own person.

CONTROLLING THE ANTS
How to Command the World

CHAPTER 9

Go to the ant, you sluggard; consider its ways and be wise.
—Proverbs 6:6

When I was growing up in the Queen City of Cincinnati, we lived near a dump or a construction site, an area right down the hill from our house. Below our house there was a basement of a supposed housing unit that was dug out, with no unit yet built. This was the favorite place we children loved to play because we would jump atop one of the mounds and climb down into the dirt where a basement was to be built. It stayed that way for years and we were hoping that the unit was never built. We would play as if we were soldiers in the dump and also acted as if we were miners looking for gold. In fact, one day I dug deep into the earth and found a ring. I never got it appraised nor did I find out whether it was real or not. It only gave me the impetus to continue digging for goodies. I just knew the necklace and the watch that matched the ring had to be nearby.

We had fun in that construction dump area even though Mom told us to stay out of it because she was sure we would get hurt, and on occasion, she was right; there was often knee bruises and hand bruises. But we never let her know. In fact, we would sneak down into the basement of our house after being covered with dirt, especially on those rainy days and we would try to clean our own clothes. We had so much fun playing in the dirt, digging in the dirt, and getting dirty in the dirt.

One of my favorite past-times was ruling the ants. I was fascinated with how they moved and how quickly they would move, especially when they were alone, thought they were under attack, or when they as a group were under attack. On occasion, I would test their individual endurance and group endurance by dropping a rock near them or within their ranks and was amazed how regimentally they moved and the courage they seemed to have in spite of the threat of a rock. I would sometimes pick them up and turn them over just to see their legs and how fast they moved, even in mid-air. I was amazed at their big heads and little bodies and the energy they exhibited at all times. I think what caused me to be so delighted with these little insects was the way they could either individually or collectively pick up objects many times their body size and weight. They would pick up a piece of bread and marshal it right to the designated location designed by the head ant.

On occasion, I would place a crumb of food in their path

or an unwrapped candy and they would just pick it up and go! How fascinating these little insects appeared going up and down valleys, through a terrain of water and rocks, and up hills. I envied them so much until I imagined, on occasion, I was one of them. I would imagine in my mind being one of them and the vast world they saw when they looked up. I could even enter their world through my own eyes and see myself looking down on them as if I were some alien giant. I loved the ant world and the organization and the cooperation they received from one another. Though they had a hierarchical society with a head ant, at the same time, they worked interdependently with each other.

One day, I decided to play a game with the ants I called "Follow the Leader" and I guess you know who the leader was. That's right, it was me. After all, I was the seventh child in a family of nine and I was tired of being the least on the totem pole. We had a rule in the house that the youngest served the eldest. Therefore, if you wanted someone to get something for you, then you asked the sibling younger than you and he or she had to do it. Well, I served six other siblings and sometimes Mom and Dad at their every behest. I was there for them when someone needed a glass of water from the kitchen. I rushed to the store, sometimes across the street and other times up the street, in between the commercials and sometimes during TV stories. One time, they even had the nerve to ask me to go to the store when Elvis Presley made his first appearance on the historic *Ed Sullivan Show* just to get a pop for them. I was even asked, though I denied their request, to go to the kitchen when the lion on *Wizard of Oz* was just getting ready to run from the wizard and jump out the window. Why, that was all of our favorite part, except for little Elmer who cried every year the lion made his traditional jump. I soon realized that slavery was not over at the time of the Emancipation Proclamation of the mid 1800s, but that I was a twentieth century slave in the Macon's home. I could not, in turn, become the master of my younger siblings because, at the time, they were too little to go to the local store by themselves. I remember one time when I asked for water they went to the nearest toilet. They were just too young. So, it didn't take me long to know that they were not there at the beckoning of my request.

I finally found a group of individuals that I could lead and instruct and if they did not follow my orders they, too, would be subjected to serious repercussions and even death. That's right, death included throwing a heavy rock on them or a brick, and if they ran I'd chase them and crush them with my little feet. I never thought the death of ants was an extreme because, after all, there were so many of them. I felt that one missing in action was not the worst of crimes though later on, when I got a little older, I discovered that ants were a part of Mother Nature's life and all existence was important and even the ants have a right to life. In fact, when I got older it became my job to protect the ant world and population. When I found them in areas they ought not to be, like the house, I would try to lead them out in single file, straight and orderly, with a piece of jam or a line of jelly poured out in front of them to lead them outdoors. Sometimes, they would follow and other times they chose their own destiny.

In following the leader to which I became the chief ant marshal and general in charge, I understood at the very beginning that none of the ants knew my potential as their leader. They were not aware of my leadership abilities and skills and how I could lead them to success and direct them to a whole area of food scrapings. I knew that if they would only follow me, I could help them end up in places where their bellies were full all the time and could create for them a spring of water trailing down from a large ledge, so they would never thirst again in their existence. And if they would only follow me, their new leader, I would return each day to give to them a fresh supply of food, water, and even exercise and recreation. So what I would do is find one ant and follow him to his tribe of ants. I would pay much attention to this ant's movement and direction. Once he arrived at the ant community, I would try to figure out the leader and watch those following him. The ant that had the most followers I assumed to be the lead ant. Soon, I would attempt to co-opt that ant by placing enticing food in front of him, not too much, only a little. I would place the food strategically in front of him and yet a distance apart. The head ant would soon be under my spell and control and finally submit to my will and way. Of course, there always stood in the back of my mind the possibility that the head ant might have to stand a slow torturing if he did not follow my directives. After all, I discovered the head ant had also at least two parts to his body and a slow death did not mean an ultimate death.

The ant was now under my spell, following the trail of bread, a little peanut butter, and some jelly. I then had to create a trench for them to stay in and I needed all the followers to align themselves perfectly within my trench. On occasion, their endurance had to be checked, and so it was the time to pour a little water from the cup into the trench. Most of them survived, but one or two of the lesser failed and so they were nicely buried under the soil and the troop continued forward. Then there were those times that I needed to see their strength. So, a big rock was placed in front of them, dug deeply in the ground so none of them could go under but only over the rock, and most of the ants passed the test. Finally, the last test, and if they passed this one, they would be victors. I reached down to see how many would climb over my hand or finger without hesitation. To my amazement they did so with much persistence, as they all passed. I knew what should be the reward for these grand and mighty ants and that was total freedom and liberation. I would pick up my remaining cup of water and toss it to the side, throw down the extra rocks that I'd picked up on the way, and take my popsicle stick and dig it deep into the soil in front of them as a sign of victory. I then walked away, knowing that my ants were ants of survival and because of my brave leadership they could pass any test in life placed before them because I was at one time their marshal and general. *Hurray to the mighty ant world!*

LIFE LESSONS YOU CAN TAKE AWAY FROM THIS STORY

The full text of Proverbs 30:24-25 reads, "There are four things which are little upon the earth, but they are exceeding wise: The ants are a people not strong, yet they prepare their meat in the summer."

God has a unique way of deflating us and taking the pride out of us. This same writer of Proverbs tells us in this passage that when we finish our education or training, we must enroll in a graduate course in the Ant College, because there is a great instructor there called the ant. The ants are great teachers: "The ants are a people not strong, yet they prepare their meat in the summer." The ants have no meteorologist to predict the coming weather. Summer is the time of opportunity to gather their food and they are very organized as a group. They are aware that the summer will not always remain. This is a great rebuke to those of us who don't know our day of opportunity, even when there are obstacles. Jeremiah, the prophet, gave a stern rebuke to those who do not recognize the time of divine visitation. "The harvest is past, the summer is ended, and we are not saved." The ants know that summer will not last always and are able to pass the tests of time.

We learn also from the ants that they have unique cooperation and coordination. When their load is too heavy for a small number of them, they have a wonderful system of summoning other ants to help, until their number is sufficient for carrying the load.

OLE BLIND GEORGE
An Intruder in the House

CHAPTER 10

Whoever loves instruction loves knowledge, but he who hates correction is stupid.

—Proverbs 12:1

I love my mother, but my mother had one major fault. She loved to take in folk, and it never mattered who they were. Mom already had us nine kids, born in ten years. Mom went to church year after year pregnant, and after ten years, the pastor wanted to know who was the new lady in church. That was my mom. My mom often talked about how she had not seen her feet in ten years due to pregnancy. Rev. Smith was so used to seeing my mother pregnant that he didn't recognize her when she started looking somewhat normal. Then, my mom and dad had the nerve to add to the nine they already had to include my five cousins who needed parental care after their parents died, which made the total count fourteen. However, when growing up I never knew of a time when we woke up in the morning that there was not an added kid from the neighborhood who was not our biological brother or cousin.

In our house, kids from the neighborhood always stayed over, of course, with their parents' permission. I told you earlier that there was Derek, who lived on the street behind our house who had only one brother and a mother, only he was too tall to get in our bed and usually slept on the floor. Then there was Steve, Jerry, Gerald, Kiser, and the rest. I always got mad when I woke up and saw these dudes at the breakfast table waiting for Dad's favorite French-fried potatoes, grits, eggs, bacon, and sausage. After all, there were fourteen of us in one small house and usually only two or three of them in their house.

I remember one person in particular—Old George. George was not a kid but a grown man. He was a friend of the family when we lived in Cincinnati and now he moved in with us in Cleveland. He was not ten or twelve years old, but about thirty-six and Old George was blind, or at least that's what they said on the street. We knew him when we were younger, right before our move to Cleveland, literally in the back of a truck. That's right! When Dad and Mom moved us to Cleveland, Dad could not afford to bring us in several cars and make several trips back and forth to our new home, the big city in the North. Therefore, he just leased a big U-Haul truck, put my mother and sister in the front seat with him, and placed the rest of us on top of a large mattress, which was on top of the furniture the day we moved. There were about six of us lying flat at the top of the inside of a U-Haul truck.

The trip from Cincinnati to Cleveland was the funniest we've ever had. At least, I thought so, or either I was too young to know what was really going on. I will never forget that day. I had worked my paper route for the last time and Mr. and Mrs. Ross had given some extra money and kissed me goodbye after placing their address in my pocket. After all, I was only twelve years old and didn't mind being treated like a child. I came home that evening and my dad was packing our belongings in the truck with a few friends. Uncle Carl showed up; he was one of my favorite uncles because when we went to his house he was always telling jokes. Sometimes, his wife, who was my Aunt Helen, would stop him when his jokes got too adult-like.

That evening, after all the furniture—the dressers, chairs, and tables—were neatly stacked almost to the very top, Dad put two mattresses on top. He started putting the young children in first, from the youngest to the eldest. The younger ones were so happy and never knew the risk they may have been taking, while the somewhat older ones were not really certain of any risk. But there was one brother who was smart enough to know that putting young kids in the back of a truck on top might not only be a little risky, but dangerous. That was my suspicious brother. He had enough sense to know that something seemed a little fishy, strange, and dangerous. He sort of feared tight spaces and going a long distance in the back of a U-Haul truck made him nervous for fear of heights

PORCH STORIES

on top of the furniture. He tried to run away that night, but Dad said, "No, you got to go." Finally, he was lifted up and laid flat on his stomach like the rest of us. I was thankful that being young we had enough room on top to at least shift and turn around if we had to. Before closing the door for the four-hour trip, Dad assured us that if we needed anything or wanted to stop at the restroom that all we had to do was hit the top of the truck and he would hear us! Of course, the little ones believed him while the suspicious older brothers knew that this not only sounded fishy, but also may have been untrue. We were off. During the entire trip we made two stops and the suspicious brother hit the top of the truck's ceiling so many times that not only did we laugh, but were most entertained by his drumming. In fact, there were times we joined in the pounding. We made it in four hours and two rest stops.

After about four years of living in Cleveland, Mom invited the family friend, Old Blind George, to live with us because he didn't have any family left in Cincinnati and his mother, Miss Carsoner, had recently died. George was really a nice brother. He was tall, dark, and quite handsome. He usually dressed in the latest fashion, prided himself in always shaving and bathing, and was not only an excellent dancer, but also sweet with the girls. That's right, whenever George was introduced to a female who he thought was attractive he would always go close to them and reach his hands out to shake their hand or embrace them but usually ended up missing their hands and reaching out to other parts of their bodies not appropriate for men to touch. Of course, it was always excusable because Old George was, after all, blind.

At one time, Old George was a well liked and a very much-respected man in the Cincinnati area. He was a professional boxer and prided himself in beating one of the greatest heavyweight champions of the world, none other than Sonny Liston. That's right! George was known in the Cincinnati area as one of the few men who had knocked down Sonny Liston, the heavyweight champion of the world, who was later beaten by Muhammad Ali, then known as Cassius Clay. That probably accounts for his charismatic personality and way with females. It was said that George was married so many times that he couldn't keep up with who his wife was at any one time. However, it was due to one of his fights that he lost his total sight, or at least we thought so in our home.

The day Old George, the thirty-six-year-old former fighter, moved in our house supposedly for a few weeks that turned out to be more like months, I just didn't like it. Here was another mouth to feed, a bed filled and a couch lost because Old George would always be around lying on it while looking at television. Though I admired Old George for his wisdom and wit, I had a problem with him being an added burden on my mom and dad. After all, my parents were still responsible for a family of fourteen.

One day, my mom and I were sitting in the kitchen and I was now nearly grown, or at least I thought so, in my own mind. I was now sixteen and had a part-time job working as a busboy at a downtown restaurant. My mom would always make us donate something to our up-keep whenever we held a job. I thought this was an excellent way to make us responsible but, at the same time, I would think that also gave us eligibility into the adult world. Being sixteen and contributing to my own livelihood made me an adult in my mind.

On this particular day, that I shall never forget, I sat down at the kitchen table to give my "adult" thoughts on the decision to continue to keep Old George in the house. After all, he was an older adult, and as of late, I did not see where he contributed one silver dime or even one red cent to help provide for his portion of the up-keep in our home. On that day, I sat with my mother to inquire as to the equity of the situation. I said to my mom, "Mom, I got a problem with Old George." And when I said that, my mother, who was usually either fixing food all day for her family or washing dishes that needed to be cleaned, as each of us would come in often and snack, and on this particular occasion she did a very unusual thing, she stopped. Mom stopped cooking, hung up the dish towel, pulled up a seat at the kitchen table, and pulled out a cigarette from the pack on the table, lit it and started to smoke while I had her undivided attention. I said, "Mom, Old George should not be living here with us!" And she inquired, "Why?" I said, "Because Old George is number one, a grown man and needs to be independent." Mom said, "Well, Old George is blind and he has no means of providing for himself." I said, as if to be the protector and defender of truth, carefully carving out my argument, as if I had studied under the tutelage of Plato or Aristotle, "Well, Mom, George can find him a job somewhere, if it's just answering phones. After all, he's only blind and not deaf."

My mom puffed on her cigarette and yet raised her eyes somewhat, as if she could not believe what she was hearing and the things that were coming out of my mouth. Mom replied, "Now, that's something awful to say about Old George. He's a kind man." But Mother allowed me to continue my argument and one-sided discussion. I said, "Mom" as if I was about to reveal something that she had really missed about George. I said, "But Mom, not only should Old George be put out immediately, but I have to tell you something that you are not aware of and that is, Old George has been lying to you all along." She glanced up and said, "Lying! Lying about what?" And that was exactly what I was waiting for her to ask in a moment of deep confusion and bewilderment. I said, "Mom, Old George is lying about the fact that he is blind. Why he's walking around with the old cane and asking people to lead him around, and touching women in inappropriate places. But the main reason why I know he's been lying to us is because the other day, I walked in on him in the living room and sure enough Old George had a book open and he was reading it." At the time, neither my mother nor I knew anything about Braille and how blind people are able to read through the touch of Braille that some books are especially published for the blind.

And even though Mom didn't know this fact and neither did I, she got up out of her chair, smashed her cigarette in the ashtray, and leaned over toward me in deep contempt and said words that have become immortal to my ears: "Son, I want you to know whether Old George can read or not, Old George is always welcome in our home. And Old George will be staying with us as long as I got breath in my body. His mother and I, when she was alive, were the best of friends and when your dad and me didn't have a dime in our pocket, his mother took care of us! Old George will always be welcomed in this home. Don't you ever uninvite George to our house. We love him and he's family." I never said a word after that, being ashamed of my thoughts.

From that day on, Old George continued to be a guest in our home, eating our food, touching ladies in inappropriate places, lying on our couch looking at TV and reading his books! Even though it was many years later that I understood the art of reading in Braille, Old George was family! A few months later, he finally moved back to Cincinnati. *The grief was over!*

LIFE LESSONS YOU CAN TAKE AWAY FROM THIS STORY

Few people can boast of having loving mothers with strong compassionate hearts for those who are troubled or in distress and in need of human kindness. Often, we focus on our own self-centered behaviors, driven by wants and desires, and fail to realize we live in an atmosphere and world of others that we are responsible for in times of need. In the Bible, Cain slew his brother Abel because of selfish reasons. Ultimately, the time of accountability came and God said to Cain, "Where is your brother, Abel?" The response of Cain was, "Am I my brother's keeper?" to which no response of God occurred because human nature and divine inspiration answers such a question with an affirmative and a loud, "Yes, we are our brothers' and sisters' keeper."

When we lose human compassion for our brothers and sisters, we have lost a sense of who we are in the realm of humanity. One only has to read Luke's gospel story of the Good Samaritan found in chapter ten, verses 25-37, to know that human compassion is a lost art today. Yet, it is something worth recovering in the twenty-first century. Unfortunately, we haven't found out how to educate people in compassion. More degrees are granted from higher educational institutions than the world has ever seen, but we, even as a nation, are filled with everything else other than compassion. With all of our technological advances in areas such as medicine and electronics, today we are no better off, morally and spiritually, than those people of long ago who first heard Jesus tell about a man who fell among thieves on the Jericho road and was healed through the compassionate efforts of a Good Samaritan. We need to recover a sense of human compassion. Where are the post-modern good Samaritans?

RUNAWAY CHILD, RUNNING WILD
An Adventure in Independence

CHAPTER 11

Success in life is not holding a good hand but playing a poor hand well.

—Danish Proverb

I shall never forget that day we left the camp in the woods. I was the runaway child, running wild! It was a beautiful day of dry summer weather and semi-heat in the Queen City of Cincinnati. Dad was fortunate enough to buy a nice home in the early 1960s in a thriving middle class black and majority white neighborhood. Our next-door neighbors to the right of us were an elderly white couple who we never met because for some odd reason the husband didn't like the Macon family. Perhaps, it was because there were too many kids who liked playing on his lawn located on a hill and corner lot. That's right, in the wintertime we used it as a hill to go down on our makeshift sleds, made out of cardboard boxes we retrieved from the local store. Or, possibly, he just didn't like the black kids in the neighborhood. We really don't know the reason,

119

all we knew is that he would yell at us and look mean at us when leaving the house in the morning with his dark business suit and white tie. He looked more like a preacher with a robust stomach and bald head than a businessman. I somewhat recall Dad telling us that he thought the man was in the mob or the Ku Klux Klan of Cincinnati. Dad did tell us to stay away from him and do what he told us. But the man's wife was very nice. I felt sorry for her because I thought about how lonely she had to be staying in that big house all day by herself while her husband was away at work. However, I thought about how nice it also was to be away from him during the day, since he appeared to be an extremely mean man. But I do remember how on a few occasions, she would see us out there playing and whisper to us to come to the door where she would have a plate of cookies. After we got our cookies she would always smile and say, "Don't say anything about these cookies to my husband." And we would just shake our heads in agreement and run off to continue our playing on her grass, especially when it became snow-filled in the winter.

The lady next door was like the Italian family who owned the fruit store where my brothers and I worked as newspaper boys. My mother had a rule in her house of nine: any boy reaching the age of five was eligible to work on People's Corner, selling newspapers. I remember my first day on the corner at the age of five. It was cold outside, and Mom made me put on extra pants, shirts, and scarves. She gave me a peck on the face and off I was on the four-mile journey from the top of Sycamore Hill to People's Corner. We started down a steep hill and up Gilmore Avenue to the top, where four main streets met at People's Corner. Here people arrived on buses that exchanged from east to west and south to north. All kinds of people: the young and the elderly, those who looked rich and affluent, the Beatles fans and the soul brothers, white, black, and whoever else, would stop at People's Corner to shop at Woolworths, eat at Joey's Hot Dog Stand and buy clothing and furniture at the local stores.

Out of all the stores on People's Corner, my favorite was Ross Fruit Store where I worked the corner, by myself, as a businessman. That's right, I thought I was the youngest businessman in Cincinnati. Of course, that was after I was promoted to that position at the tender age of nine. Before that time, I was under the supervision of my two older brothers, Rick, first known as the Big Bad Wolf, and Walt, known as the Mellow Brother who promised he would never eat another plate of beans in his life. Of course, one day we slipped in on Walt without notice, and lo and behold, he was sitting at a restaurant counter eating a hot bowl of pork 'n' beans soup!

Rick was a tough businessman. When he hired us, his little brothers, he held a Mafia attitude, and at times, was no different from the Mafia Boss, Jimmy Hoffa. He would shake us down literally every evening. We would go from the William Howard Taft Elementary School, down the hill, and up the other hill to People's Corner and walk down to Gilbert Avenue's newspaper stand and sell papers. I remember this so well because I shared a corner with Phil, my other older brother. When the evening shift ended about 7 p.m., the Big Bad Wolf would come and get the collection from the sale of the papers. Rick would tell us before the shift began that we could keep all the tips but usually when the shift was over he would take sales' dollars, tips, and all. So Phil and I got smart! We started hiding the tips, but every evening we literally had to shake down. That's right, Rick would make us jump up and down and if he heard any change, we had to give it up to this Mafia-type boss. Soon we got even smarter and started hiding the money in secret compartments in our inner coats and jackets. We would cut out the interior of the coat and hide the money, but usually Rick would still come by and find the secret hiding places with the money. We soon wised up and decided to hide the money under the bubble gum machine and newspaper stand. Rick still was smart enough to tell us he was leaving and we could walk home, only to hide around the corner and wait and see where we would go and pick up our loot. He would return and demand all receipts in cash.

One day, he beat us around and I threw his money in the street water drain and told him later we were robbed. Rick was one of the funniest mobsters I'd ever met because usually when we got beat up, which was really no beating at all, he made sure he never really hurt us because if mom had found any markings on us, Rick would have the devil to pay. At the end of the day, I loved my mobster brother because he really wasn't a criminal; just a shrewd businessman whom we sometimes outsmarted and other times got caught.

It was not many years after, that I got promoted to work on the main street of People's Corner for Walt. I had my own paper route. Walt was a better businessman than Rick and used no mobster style tactics. He was responsible for his own corner, and on many occasions, Walt would do whatever necessary to sell his papers. I've seen him stop major traffic to sell one paper. On occasion, he would even stop a moving bus to hop on when a person waved to him through the window to bring them a newspaper. Another time, there was a four-way car accident caused by Walt who ran in the street to sell his paper. He was the biggest and best young hustler of papers in town.

Walter would always talk about never eating beans again in his life because our family was large and relatively poor and the money was limited. My dad was the only one working outside the household because Mom was busy raising all nine of us kids. Growing up, I remember that every night Mother would feed us with plenty of protein, a big bowl of beans and fat back. We ate every kind of bean America could produce, every night! We had pork and beans, pinto beans, black-eye beans, red beans, string beans, and so many more kinds of beans. I guess my mother also thought as long as our bellies were full and we had our protein we would be fine.

Walt was the liberationist of the family and decided he would never eat beans again in his life once he could provide his own means through the paper sale business. Often, we would find him around the corner or across the street eating hot dogs and hamburgers at the deli. He was also good at going down to the local White Castle Restaurant where you could get four hamburgers for less than a half dollar. Or, at least, we thought that's what he paid because Walter was a shrewd businessman. We always boasted of his multi-faceted businesses. That's right! Not only did he sell newspapers, but also he was the local two cents empty soda bottle collector. He would go down to the local grocery store and get a cart and go all around the city, picking up empty soda bottles to return them for this monetary exchange. It was never beneath Walt to look for lost change in the streets and pick it up. He was always nice to his customers, hoping to get a tip for the sale of newspapers.

One day, Walt, the businessman, decided to retire from the newspaper business and work in the furniture store as a stock boy. He gave me all rights and privileges to the corner he was working. I will never forget that day! It was like he gave me the keys to a new business. He included the stand that held the papers and the brick we put on the papers to keep them from flying away and the other brick he would stand on to keep his feet from getting cold. That's right, there was a brick that kept our feet from getting cold in the winter! We would get a brick and take it into Mr. and Mrs. Ross' fruit stand and she would place it in the oven and wrap it in a cloth and give it to us to take out to the corner and stand on it. This process was done often during the shift. I soon became a businessman and held all rights to the corner that Walter had been responsible for. However, I never sold the large number of papers like Walt because I never had the courage to step out in the middle of traffic to sell a paper. I was really mediocre and sometimes rather terrible. On occasion, I would receive the threat of losing my job by the head distribution manager of the paper company if I did not sell more papers, but I was never really worried because I knew my personal charisma would keep me going and in favor with the boss. After all, everyone told me I had the cutest little dimples in town and the saddest frown of any little boy, and I knew how to use both of them.

The day I was about to receive my pink slip and be booted from the job, one central event occurred that saved my job as a newspaper boy. The occasion was the assassination of John F. Kennedy, the President of the United States of America. I will never forget that day. I heard the news and people were crying everywhere as we watched the assassination of this young president who both Negroes and whites admired. This was a young, nice family and the death of the President's younger child had occurred not long before this incident. On that day, we all rushed to our corners to sell our newspapers. The papers were late in coming because the Cincinnati Post newspaper company could not print enough of them, knowing they would sell out early. Sure enough, they did and all of us who were newspaper boys were big hits that day because people yelled from everywhere requesting a copy of the paper. That day, I retained my position because my numbers were up, again!

However, I walked home happy because I did not lose my job, but sad because I retained it due to the awful death of the young president. I was personally saddened because I voted for the president. That's right! The year of President Kennedy's election, I was in an elementary class where the kids were in a debate as to who they would vote for as that year's president. We were shown a picture of Richard Nixon and John F. Kennedy and viewed the actual televised debate. We saw it on a black and white T.V. When I looked at it, I was not impressed by the troublesome looking, deep black-haired Nixon who served as vice-president of the country. But I loved the smiles and sincere, relaxed look of the young John F. Kennedy. After watching the debate we were asked to vote right there in class. Naturally, I voted for Kennedy and heard how young JFK, that's what they called him, helped out Martin Luther King, Jr. who was once in a Birmingham jail, during the civil rights period. I would tell you more about that, but that's another porch story!

Mr. and Mrs. Ross were my favorite people in the whole world. They owned and worked a fruit stand and store for years. I thought for years they were Italians, but later on, one evening, I discovered they may have been Jewish. They were two of the kindest people in the world, who did not have children. I really don't know if they were married or just brother and sister. I do know that Billy Ross, that was his name, loved to go to the local pub. On one occasion, I followed him into the pub and tried to act as if I was there trying to sell my papers. I remember seeing Billy order a drink and leave. Soon, I would follow him in and out of the pub without him knowing. But one time I got caught! It was an afternoon, and really I could not hide in the pub this day because there were only a few people in there at this early afternoon time. So Billy just yelled to me to come over to the bar and with my small self I threw my load of papers on one bar stool and jumped up next to Billy's seat. Billy said to the bartender, "Give him a cherry drink with a cherry." The bartender pulled out a champagne cup, poured cherry soda in it, and plopped in a juicy red cherry. From that day on, I came in and jumped up on the stool, laid my papers on the stool next to me, and ordered my daily cherry soda, all by myself. This continued until one day a policeman came in while I was drinking. The policeman was ready to arrest every one in the pub, seeing that they were serving a minor, until he was told it was just soda pop. However, from that day on all the drinks dried up and I was never allowed to sit at the bar. Although, I was saddened by the decision, I was relieved that nobody went to jail that day!

I discovered that the Ross family was Jewish when one

day a white man who looked more like a businessman with a dark suit, white shirt, dark tie, and hat came up to me on the corner and ordered a newspaper. I gave it to him and asked for my money. He called me a nigger and said he wasn't going to give a nigger anything. I ran into the fruit store and told Mr. Ross what happened. Mr. Ross looked more like Popeye the Sailorman and always wore a cap and smoked a pipe. He ran out to tell the man to give me my money and to explain why he refused to give me my money. The man refused to give a full explanation and Mr. Ross started to walk furiously into the store as if to get a pistol to deal with this situation. The man followed Mr. Ross into the store with his briefcase and called Mr. Ross a nasty Jewish name and admonished him for being a nigger lover. I thought that was terrible enough, but the man then had the audacity to lift up his briefcase and proceeded to hit Billy upside the head with the briefcase. Billy instantly lifted up his left hand to prevent from getting hit and with the sweetest right hook and the strength of Popeye, hit the man on the right jaw and instantly, as in a Muhammad Ali and Joe Frazier prize fight, he went down. When the man got up, I could see him picking up his briefcase and running out the door. From that day on, Billy was my hero, as he looked at me and said, "No one will ever call you that name and never insult me like that." Mrs. Ross gave me a piece of fruit and told me to go back selling papers and she walked Billy back to the rear of the store to make sure he was not hurt. I knew then what it meant to be the defender of justice.

I said all of that because that was the same day I decided to leave home. Later that day, my mother ordered me to bed early for something I really did not do, but because I was the oldest in the room of the occurrence, I was held responsible for not controlling the actions of my little brothers. To this day, I don't remember what it was they did wrong. I decided that day I was going to leave and set up camp down the street in the woods. I will never forget that evening. I slipped off with Raymond, my younger brother, as my new recruit, to carry my supplies. We got a few dishes, forks, spoons, and knives from the kitchen and a large bed sheet. I knew how to set up camp only because I was familiar with the woods below our house and had been there before. That evening we were off just before dark where I keenly identified an area in the woods that I would soon make my permanent residence. I pulled a few tree limbs over and spread the sheet over the branches. Then I put all my wares on the ground after clearing out an area to sleep on. Soon, it started to get dark, and the animals for some odd reason sounded louder that night. Raymond saw the darkness and heard the animals, and we even thought we heard a wolf growl. It probably was a dog but Ray got scared and thought it was time that, he, if not both of us, should leave camp. He said, "Brother, is there anything else I can do for you? You know it's getting late and I got to make sure I'm home before dark and the streetlights come on." I said, "No, Ray, I'm fine. I got my camp, my pots, and pans to fix my food in the morning and I'll be living out here in the woods, so don't tell anyone."

Ray left and within three minutes the darkness covered my campground. The noise from the animals and insects seemed to intensify; the wind started blowing and the trees started swaying. Some unidentifiable sounds were heard, goose bumps appeared on my arm, my nappy hair seemed to rise, the moon got brighter and the stars were more prominent. I knew it was about time for me to close up camp and get out of the woods as fast as I could. The strange thing about it was that my feet took on a mind of their own and my arms started swaying and I had no control over my eyes because all I could see was home, a warm bed, and a room filled with my brothers and sisters.

Without a second thought, I got up and followed all the faculties of my body and left the camp, the pots and pans and bed sheet over the limbs and branches and I couldn't get out of the woods fast enough. A strange fear caught hold of me and, like Dorothy in "The Wizard of Oz," all I could think about was, "There's no place like home." I arrived home, a twenty-minute trip that seemed to me to take less than three minutes. I took off so fast that I cared less of what was left behind. I was home, at last.

The next day, I went back to my camp early in the morning only to find nothing! That's right, all of my mother's wares were gone, including the sheet. The only thing I knew was it's good to have a brother you can trust for confidence because if mother ever had discovered that I set up camp and ran away with her kitchen utensils and some of her bed linens, I would never see the light of day again. All in all, I was very glad the day we left the camp because the run away child had returned home!

Life Lessons You Can Take Away From this Story

As children, we often have various experiences and our parents are either misunderstood by us or they misunderstand us. However, running away from problems instead of facing the problems should not ever become an option. We will discover that the protective care of a loving parent, willing to engage in an open conversation of those misunderstandings, will lead to resolution of many of the problems that we as children may have in viewing our parents. At the end of the day, because of God's great law in His Ten Commandments that says, "Honor thy father and thy mother" the child will ultimately have to return home "that thy days may be long upon the earth."

THE NIGHT I GOT SAVED
Doing the Holy Dance

CHAPTER 12

Verily, verily, I say unto you, Except one be born anew, he cannot see the Kingdom of God.

—Jesus Christ (John 3:3)

Everybody should know the day or night that they got saved. Being saved is a very powerful moment and a transcending experience, especially, in its supernatural happening. I remember when I was spiritually saved at the First Baptist Church in Mt. Auburn, a special section located in Cincinnati, Ohio. The church overlooked the entire downtown area and was located at the top of the highest hill known as Sycamore Hill. The Rev. B.W. Smith was just preaching up a storm and sing-songing his sermon in the tradition of the old black preacher and the slave church. Everybody was up on his or her feet with shouts of praise and one old mother of the church went into a dance of praise. We call that shouting and church at its best. After all, if no one is shouting and the preacher cannot lead them into the frenzy or holy dance, then the preacher has not really done his job on Sunday. Look at them: Ms. Fuse hanging onto her fur coat with the fox head flying, and Ms. Kimbrel crying with tears pouring down her face looking all ugly, and Deacon Collier yelling at the preacher with his exultant "Amen," "Say it, Reverend," "Bring it on home, pastor." Boy, they were having church while we little ones were laughing and mocking the shouters!

It was one of those kinds of Sunday morning services that we were having when the preacher lowered his voice and the congregants sat down in a silent hush, while the choir began to moan in a spirit of holiness, that the preacher began to talk about who wanted to get saved. His voice was low and his eyes were piercing, and looking around the church room, he asked, "Who wants to be saved?" And then he added, "Whosoever will let them come, even if you are a little child. The Bible says a child shall lead the way." That was my brother's opening. He was nine years old and a little chubby for his age but he accepted the invitation to and marched later on to be baptized. He got up off his bench and forward he marched to the front. Nobody knew he was going to be saved but me because earlier in the service Ray told me that he was going to be saved and baptized. After all, he liked the little small swimming pool in the basement of the church and thought he could hold his breath long enough to be dipped and come up new. He even challenged me to go with him when he went but I was a little afraid and told him that if he went first, I would follow.

Ray went up first with his chubby self and boy, did the people like it when nine-year-old Ray walked to the front of First Baptist Church! They all started shouting again and my mother started crying and Daddy seemed to have encouraged him on with the smile on his proud face. I saw that and said to myself that Ray wasn't going to get all the praise to himself. So I mustered up enough strength to get out of my seat and go forward. After all, I was the older brother and he should not be baptized before me. I started to the front but noticed that there was still enough shout for me, too. People started praising God and the pastor started waving his hands in the air and Daddy and Momma gave me the affirmation, or at least I thought it was for me. When I got to the front, I looked to the back and discovered that all that shouting was not just for me, but because my baby brother, Elmer, was following after me, in his big brother's footsteps. He was so small and short that few people could see him but evidently he was tall enough to get all the praise. We all three were saved on the same day, but only two were baptized. That's right, even though three walked up, only two were brave enough to go under the water.

I remember that day as if it was yesterday. On Saturday night we got ready for Sunday service. It was the first Sunday of the month, a special time in the black church experience, and at the evening service we would all be baptized with a large crowd looking on. We all had to wear white shirts, white pants, and white socks. All of us went to the room for dressing and we were ready with our triple white. Ray looked good but his shirt was too tight, Elmer was fine but his pants were too big and me, why I looked like a black angel coming down from Heaven with everything just right. I even had the nerve to put on a black belt for the occasion.

At the church there was a line of towels on the floor leading from the room we were in to the baptismal pool in the basement, with a line of people and the old mothers of the church with all their white on. The deacons were singing and the people were spectators. Ray went first, up the steps and then down the steps, and he and the preacher stood center stage. The preacher yelled, "I baptize you" and the people started falling out. Ray went down, grabbed hold of his nose and back up he came, and Ray was now saved. It was my turn and I knew I would soon be on center stage and the same performance from the audience would ultimately be my lot. I went down, but to show Ray that I had more courage, I didn't hold my nose, I just held my breath and just as cool, calm, and collected as an alley cat, I came up with the assurance that I had been saved.

It was now Elmer's turn, the little one who could hardly be escorted up the steps, then down. When it was time to descend in the water like an eel in the sea, Elmer screamed and squirmed so badly until my dad, Deacon Macon, had to stop the baptismal service and tell the pastor, "Let him out," because he wasn't quite ready. Ray and I were looking and peeping out the door and when Elmer performed we went into a laughing rage, but Elmer didn't care. All he knew was that he was not willing to swallow up a lake on that day. When he got back to the room to change his wet clothes, Ray and I couldn't stop laughing. It was the greatest show on earth and little Elmer was the key clown of the circus. What a day it was when we got saved at the little church on the hill, First Baptist Church of Auburn Avenue in Cincinnati, Ohio.

After I got saved, I learned the holy dance. I didn't learn the dance at the First Baptist Church but at an uncle's Holiness Church. I was touched and excited to see all the folk dancing. My sister Helen knew how to dance. She knew how to fall out and roll on the floor. I was very observant because after she fainted in the spirit and rolled on the floor, she achieved the attention of the robe coverers. Those were the older ladies in white who covered you from being exposed, especially the ladies. The night I learned the holy dance was the night I observed keenly. I watched how they crossed their legs and shuffled to the right and then to the left and spun in counter-clockwise fashion. I closed one eye and kept the other one open and then I grabbed my pant leg and danced in the spirit. The music was just right and the pastor encouraged us all to be caught up in the "free spirit of the Lawd." I was caught up until suddenly I almost slipped and lost my balance. I picked myself up and composed myself and tried it again, and again, and again! This was good old-fashioned church and we all were praising the Lord until the pastor said, "That's enough, let's all sit down." And so I did because I just knew I had been saved and the expression of that was dancing in the spirit. I was saved, sanctified, and filled with the Spirit because I had been baptized. And now I could dance to prove it!

LIFE LESSONS YOU CAN TAKE AWAY FROM THIS STORY

True salvation is more than profession in a saving faith in Christ Jesus, but includes a living experience. The old folk of yesterday had a saying, "If you have been born again, you ought to show some sign." Therefore, if one has been saved, there ought to be an outward expression of water baptism and inward joy, sometimes expressed in holy dancing and a shout. This manifestation of inward change ought to be seen in one's walk, talk, and behavior. If it is spirit-led, then there are no embarrassments or hesitation in expressing that manifestation.

I believe today in the plan of salvation and that with its confession comes the true spirit life with many forms of expressions. A personal trust in Jesus Christ as one's Lord is merely this:

1. Accept the fact that you are a sinner, and that you have broken God's law. The Bible says in Ecclesiastes 7:20: *"For there is not a just man upon earth that doeth good, and sinneth not."* Romans 3:23 says, *"For all have*

sinned and come short of the glory of God.”

2. Accept the fact that there is a penalty for sin. The Bible states in Romans 6:23: *“For the wages of sin is death…”*

3. Accept the fact that you are on the road to hell. Jesus Christ said in Matthew 10:28: *“And fear not them which kill the body, but are not able to kill the soul: but rather fear him which is able to destroy both soul and body in hell.”*

The Bible says in Revelation 21:8: *“But the fearful and unbelieving, and abominable, and murderers, and whoremongers and sorcerers, and idolaters, and all liars, shall have their part in the lake which burneth with fire and brimstone: which is the second death.”*

4. Accept the fact that you cannot do anything to save yourself! The Bible states in Ephesians 2:8-9: *“For by grace are ye saved through faith: and that not of yourselves: it is a gift of God. Not of works, lest any man should boast.”*

5. Accept the fact that God loves you more than you love yourself, and that He wants to save you from hell. *“For God so loved the world, that He gave His only*

begotten Son, that whosoever believeth in Him should not perish, but have everlasting life" (John 3:16).

6. I believe with these facts in mind and heart, if we repent of our sins, believe on the Lord Jesus Christ and pray and ask Him to come into our hearts and save us, then we are saved that very moment.

The Bible says in the book of Romans 10:9, 13: *"That if thou shalt confess with thy mouth the Lord Jesus, and shalt believe in thine heart that God hath raised Him from the dead, thou shalt be saved." "For whosoever shall call upon the name of the Lord Jesus shall be saved."*

If you are willing to trust Christ as your Savior, please pray the following prayer:

Heavenly Father, I realize that I am a sinner and that I have sinned against you. For Jesus Christ sake, please forgive me of all my sins. I now believe with all of my heart that Jesus Christ died, was buried, and rose again for me. Lord Jesus, please come into my heart, save my soul, change my life, and fill me with your Holy Ghost today and forever. Amen.

PART FOUR

IS JUSTICE JUST FOR US?

———— Is Justice Just for Us? ————

WE LIVE IN a great nation that was founded upon great principles. There is no place like the United States of America. Few of us would want to live in any other place in the world. Our history in this nation is exceptional. However, America, too, comes with its historical pains and challenges. Some of them have existed from its very inception as a nation. There has been what so many have called "The Color Line" problem or racism.

If America is going to continue to be great, she will have to eradicate all forms of discriminatory acts through legislation. To repeal one law and to enact another to reinforce a system that ultimately oppresses all is not only unjust but also immoral. America was based upon moral and theocratic principles. God has for centuries ruled divinely and led our nation. If America is to continue on this path, she must not only rethink her laws, but she must turn to her Lord and Saviour, Jesus Christ.

There are so many stories of injustice in America that we could not contain them all in one book of Porch Stories. However, these too are stories that need to be told so that incidents of injustice can be a thing of the past. Justice is not always justice for all and may be justice for just a few.

JUSTICE AT A DISTANCE
When Justice is Not For All

CHAPTER 13

The story is told of a pilot in Ft. Worth, Texas, who had his own two-engine plane. He had flown many, many hours and was very capable of flying his aircraft. He got up in his aircraft one day and began to fly the wide blue skies when he suddenly found himself eighty to ninety miles away from the Dallas/Ft. Worth airport. While he was flying, he began to hear something in the cockpit of his airplane that he had never heard before. It was a little twitching noise. He heard what could be described only as a "ttt-tt-ttt-tt-ttt-tt" in his cockpit and didn't know what it was. The pilot became extremely worried because the noise was annoying and he didn't know what it was. Finally, he called back to the tower to explain what was happening and where it happened inside the plane. He explained to the man in the tower, "I'm hearing a noise in my cockpit and I can't figure out what it is that's causing this problem. I hear it, but I've never heard it before."

The man in the tower tells the pilot to check some things such as the instrumentation, lights and other gadgets.

Finally, the man in the tower said, "Go over and check a certain instrument which normally has a red light on." Well, sure enough, when the pilot flipped that switch, the light did not come on. That was the hot wire going to the engine from the generator in the airplane that makes the engines run.

The tower radioed back, "You've got a problem." The pilot said, "You're telling me?" The man in the tower said "I'm going to tell you what you have in your cockpit. You have a rat in your airplane." The pilot said, "What do you mean?" The man in the tower said, "Rats will climb up into the cockpit and when you get at a certain altitude, they will search out the hot things in the airplane to chew on and eat."

The man in the tower said, "He is eating your hot wires." The pilot said, "My God, can I make it back to Dallas?" The response was, "I wouldn't even try it." The pilot said, "Well, what shall I do?" The man in the tower said, "I want you to take your aircraft, and I want you to go to an altitude that you've never been before." He said, "Pull the throttle back and go to 12,000 feet above your normal flying altitude." The pilot did so and his aircraft began trembling as if it was about to cave in when suddenly the noise in the cockpit stopped.

When the pilot brought his aircraft back down and landed at the airport, sure enough, as they began to search his aircraft and took the panel off the top of his cockpit there lying on the panel was a dead rat. The pilot asked, "Why in the world did that rat die in the plane?" The response was, "Rats cannot live at certain altitudes."

LIFE LESSONS YOU CAN TAKE AWAY FROM THIS STORY

I believe in complete integration for all and never segregation of any. We must not think that just an acknowledgement of the social problem of racism is a healthy approach to its issues and that reflection on the past is enough. However, both legal and religious analysis of the future is appropriate, when we are faced with the problem of segregation in a community to maintain a progressive America. As such, we must recognize our responsibility to share the story of what has historically occurred in America to Americans, both good and bad, and in particular to black Americans. If one becomes offended by that truth then liberation has already begun because the Bible says, "The truth shall set you free."

It must be our intent as individuals, and a nation, to help get rid of the rats of segregation and racism in the cockpit of America. We must order America to higher heights of morality through equality and fairness toward all. The rats of racism and discrimination must die. We hope that a renewed legal system and religious values become the 12,000 additional feet needed to extinguish them forever!

IS THE JUSTICE SYSTEM FOR US?
The Need for Moral Laws

CHAPTER 14

"And judgment is turned away backward, and justice standeth afar off: for truth is *fallen in the street, and equity cannot enter.*"

—Isaiah 59:13

Just think about it: when we look at the symbol of justice in America, it is represented in the form of a woman statue, located outside of the U.S. Supreme Court building in Washington, D.C. She is blind-folded which leads us to believe that justice in America is blind toward ethnicity, economics and other variables. Also, she holds a scale in one hand, which symbolizes that justice in America should not favor one person over another on the basis of irrelevant characteristics such as color. In other words, the same laws ought to apply to all equally. The scale presupposes the belief that treatment under the law ought to be according to what is due a person on the same grounds. However, the reality is that many African Americans along with other minorities are not treated fairly when crimes are committed in the justice system of America.

Dr. Tony Evans, Senior Pastor of Oak Cliff Bible Fellowship in Dallas, Texas, tells the story of how many people discriminate in the area of education. He explained, that whether you have a PhD or a GED, we all have come through the same door. God did not look at our resume before He brought individuals into the kingdom. God didn't see whether a person had a BS, MBA, or PhD. He wanted to give everybody the right BA – born again. Our education, says Dr. Evans, or lack of it, doesn't make us any better or worse in God's sight. If this is the case, America needs to learn a lesson from God.

LIFE LESSONS YOU CAN TAKE AWAY FROM THIS STORY

As African Americans in today's world and time, several questions have haunted both my son and me: "Has judgment been turned backward and justice stood afar off for minorities in America? Has truth fallen in the street where fairness cannot enter? Is the justice system fair for all Americans and in particular, Blacks and Hispanic males?" These questions seek to understand the truth as to whether or not America's justice and legal system is set up to help or penalize the individual communities and other minorities.

We believed that the greatest benefit of living in a free and democratic society has to do with *liberty and justice for all.* However, after looking at the criminal justice system in

America it is easy to begin questioning whether justice is truly impartial and fairly distributed to all who are living in America regardless of race, creed, or color.

The criminal justice system itself raises serious questions when hearing the devastating statistic that more than fifty percent of our prisoners and probationers are African American and Hispanic males. It is African American males who represent less than 6% of America's population, but are 50% of those on America's death row. This creates a kind of mistrust toward those who call themselves fair distributors of justice in the criminal system.

In short, while people of color represent a minority in the United States population, they are a majority in terms of these prison populations. A number of inequities are seen in policing, driving while black, legal representation, litigation procedures, and sentencing. However, the Bible informs us that when moral people take oversight in judicial and political offices in creation of laws that seek to dispense justice equally and fairly to all people, the whole world benefits. The Scripture bears this out especially when looking at a statement made by the author of Second Samuel regarding King David who was king of Israel. II Samuel 8:15 says: *"And David reigned over all Israel; and David executed judgment and justice unto all his people."*

Notwithstanding, you can be sure that all who are in judicial offices today are not all moral people. It is this truth that raises the question: *"Is the justice system just or fair for* all?" The long years of a negative history in America, which details 244 years of black slavery and over 100 years of legalized segregation and inequity, suggest that America's justice system was created to disenfranchise blacks.

Yet, Christianity teaches that God loves all people and He expects all to relate to one another righteously. According to Apostle Paul's letter to the church at Galatia, *"There is neither Jew nor Greek, there is neither bond nor free, there is neither male nor female: for ye are all one in Christ Jesus"* (Galatians 3:28).

Therefore, ought not justice to be dispensed in America fairly among all people regardless of race, creed or color, or with a degree of evenhandedness? After all, justice in America coincides with Christian belief in rightness. Christianity affirms that God is color-blind in terms of just and right treatment toward humanity. Race, color, and creed do not matter to Him. God is a God of inclusiveness and is not a respecter of persons. And so ought America to show impartiality when it comes down to the fair distribution of justice.

We, as a nation, must believe that both the church that represents the Lord, and the legal system of America that represents the law can make a difference in speaking out against the inequities through advocacy, litigation, voting and citizenship principles when they are joined together.

However, we further believe that the pathetic imbalance of law observed in the criminal justice system today in

America is inextricably tied to imbalances in the political, economic, and educational systems, and other institutions of racism that still exist in our society. Hence, justice is not for all; it is unholy and unjust and creates negative nuances in the family. Also, other ethnic groups such as Arabs, and now the Mexican communities, are experiencing injustices within America's legal and penal system. They, too, find themselves incarcerated and discriminated against at unprecedented and alarming rates.

You will discover that injustice in America is a systemic problem and the American justice system will need to be overhauled. It is easy to see that social justice has not been achieved in America and the passage of a Civil Rights Bill and Voting Rights Act of the 1960's does not guarantee equality and fairness. It is our opinion, as observers in this American society, that both the Church and the Law or legal systems have a responsibility to correct the injustices. Also, the Christian church must do a better job in defining how justice occurs from a theological perspective, while the court system must do a better job at implementing laws and practices equally. Also, Christians who represent our Lord Jesus Christ must emphasize—in words and in deeds—how injustice is intolerable and how all social evils hurt not only particular ethnic groups, but also all people.

And "What does the Lord and law require of us?" This, too, has a reliable answer. The prophet Micah simply stated it this way: *"He hath showed thee, O man, what is good, and what doth the Lord require of thee, but to do justly, and to love mercy, and to walk humbly with thy God?"* (Micah 6:8).

IN TROUBLE WITH THE LAW
DNA Has Made a Difference

CHAPTER 15

"Man sent to prison and files suit: Green jailed for rape he didn't commit" was the title of an article in the Cleveland Metro section of the *Plain Dealer* on May 16, 2003. It tells the sad story of a man imprisoned for a crime he did not commit. Michael Green was a man imprisoned for 13 years for rape and the law totally dismissed the charges after Michael's DNA testing proved that he didn't attack a terminally ill cancer patient at the local Cleveland Clinic Center Hotel. In fact, a suit by Green's attorney claimed that investigators botched the case by improperly suggesting information to the victim that helped her pick out Green's picture in a photo lineup and fabricated evidence used to arrest and convict Green. When the victim was initially given a photo spread, she failed to identify Green as the rapist. Green immediately went voluntarily to the Clinic's security office, offered to submit blood and saliva samples and he requested a police line up and a DNA test. Yet, he was still in trouble with the law, handcuffed, tried and imprisoned for thirteen years for a crime he did not commit.

How many other men are in trouble with the law for crimes they did not commit, except for being born black or Hispanic? Today, there are so many men like Green who have been victimized by America's justice system. As a first year law student at FAMU in Orlando, I was in the law library one day and met a black brother who I will call John. He informed me how he had been faced with legal injustices throughout his life. John was a thirty-nine year old black male who shared with me how on at least five different occasions he had seen justice pass him by. Because of the injustice he faced, he dedicated twenty years of his life to researching the law. John further stated how he felt the need to safeguard himself from those who enforced the laws unfairly such as lawyers, police officers and courtroom judges.

John was not only an African American male, but also a husband and father who felt that there is no justice for a black man in most situations. He informed me how he encountered the biggest example of injustice one night when he was at a local store where both he and the manager got into a heated argument because the manager was flirting with his wife. Finally, one of the store's clerks called the police. When the white policemen came to the scene they immediately threw him to the ground and handcuffed him without hearing his side of the story. They began to question him without even reading him his Miranda rights. Then the police allowed the store manager to pick him up off the ground and punch him while being handcuffed and then they all commenced to toss him back to the ground several times while collectively kicking him.

John cried real tears while telling me his painful story. Suddenly, I noticed how he quickly wiped away those tears and said, "The law should be fair! The law and justice ought to be one and the same for all people regardless of color." He then continued to explain how he believed that he was given no rights that night because he was a black male in America. John recounted how there was no threat of violence to the store manager, only a verbal warning to stop flirting with his wife. He closed his discussion by saying, "Justice in America is a lie for black folk." Sadly, I left believing that John may have been right.

LIFE LESSONS YOU CAN TAKE AWAY FROM THIS STORY

There are many black men like John who have experienced this type of injustice. We do not have to go back to slave days to realize what has been going on in America with black males. It was nearly two decades ago, on April 29, 1992, that an all-white jury had acquitted all four of the white police officers on trial for using excessive force against Los Angeles motorist Rodney King. A year earlier, Rodney King was stopped by the Los Angeles Police Department and mercilessly brutalized by white policemen who should have merely arrested King for a routine traffic stop. Thanks to an area resident's videotape, this black man, who was being beaten with more than fifty baton blows, several kicks, and paralyzing electric laser shocks was later vindicated. This defenseless black male was hospitalized and left with a bruised kidney, eleven skull fractures, and brain damage that still affects him today. It became apparent that justice is not for all, especially when you are a black man like Rodney King who was stopped for a routine traffic violation.

During the same year that all four white police officers were acquitted of using excessive force against Rodney King, a black man named Donald Coleman, who tossed a Molotov cocktail into a 7-Eleven store, was sentenced to nineteen years and eight months in prison for his participation in the riot that broke out in 1992. Justice and equality make strange bed partners when it comes down to some black people.

Is justice for all when you are already in trouble? It certainly does not appear to be so when one considers what happened six years after the Rodney King incident in Pittsburgh. A black man named Johnny E. Gammage was pulled over by the police for "driving erratically," and was beaten to death because those policemen said he was "out of control." They, too, were acquitted. I am not sure if the number "four" is a magic number when it comes to police brutality, but it was for four New York police officers who put more than forty bullets in a black man named Amadou Diallo after mistaking him for a suspect. They, too, were acquitted on February 24, 2000. In Cincinnati, an unarmed teenager named Timothy Thomas was shot and killed by a Cincinnati policeman and he, too, was acquitted of his crime. It certainly appears that the legal system continues to fail to protect the values and interests of people if they happen to be of African American or Hispanic descent.

Yet, in this day and age, one wonders how those representing the legal and safety force can be so unjust in their decisions and actions towards minorities. It goes to show that America has more work to do if it is to become the type of society that is fair toward everyone.

PART FIVE

WHEN THE LORD IS INVOLVED

—— WHEN THE LORD IS INVOLVED ——

OUR ATTITUDES ARE formed by the events that make up our experiences and one's faith statement. We become strong or weak depending on how we react to these experiences and our dependence on God. Most people have more choices about how they react to life than they realize. Poverty makes some people bitter, but others stronger because they have to fight circumstances just to stay alive. When things and events control us, we become a mere extension of them. In a way, this reduces us to the level of a thing or an event. However, we have the power to use experiences as tools and God as a guide. We can learn from both them and the Lord when He is on our side and speaking to us. We can grow to be greater than our background and higher than our circumstances, or we can become slaves to them.

WHEN THE LORD IS ON YOUR SIDE
The Wrong Solution for Hiccups

CHAPTER 16

The story is told of a young man who stopped at the drug store to get some hiccup medicine. He asked the drug store clerk, "Do you have anything good for the hiccups?" The clerk reached over and slapped the man up side the head! It took a minute to get his balance. The man looked at the clerk again. "Sir, do you have anything for the hiccups?" "Man, have you still got the hiccups?" "I never did have them," he yelled. "My wife in the car has the hiccups." I said to myself, "Thank God, the Lord has been most patient with both those who have been oppressed by the law as well as the oppressor of the law!"

Another story is told of a little boy who was in the grocery store one day with his mother. He saw a big box of cherries, and he stared at them. He wanted some badly. The grocer said, "Go ahead, Billy, get a handful of cherries if you want them." Billy responded, "Uh-h-h." The grocer figured the reason Billy did not take the cherries was because his mother had instructed him not to. So the grocer asked Mrs.

Smith, "Would it be alright if Billy has a handful of cherries?" She said, "Sure, Billy go ahead." Billy said, "Uh-h-h." Finally, the grocer reached over, got a handful of cherries, crammed them into Billy's pocket and said, "Now there, Billy." When they got outside, Billy's mother said, "Billy, you embarrassed me today. The grocer said you could have the cherries, and I told you that you could have them. Why didn't you get the cherries?" Billy looked up into his mother's face and said, "His hand is bigger than mine!" Thank God, the Lord's hands are bigger than ours and when He is on our side, the Lord will dispense justice mixed with mercy for all!

LIFE LESSONS YOU CAN TAKE AWAY FROM THIS STORY

Throughout American history, no race of people has been more subjected to such cruel and systematic suffering as black people whose only apparent sin is being blackened by nature's sun. It is because of our differences that blacks have been subjugated to a place and position of inferiority in America. They have been mistreated and been called every thing other than children of God.

There are even those earlier white scholars who tried to argue that the Bible and God both ordained and condemned blacks to be slaves of the human race. But if the Bible is not clear about anything else, it is explicit about the fact that God made of one blood all nations of persons to dwell upon the earth together (Acts 17:26).

It is sad to say, but in all the literature stretching back into the dusty volumes of antiquity, black people have been referred to in negative and demeaning ways. In fact, many black heroes and heroines have been written out of the history books. When they were included they became a convenient tool to portray them as less than human. American history had assigned them to the basement of the human family.

The many years of inhumane treatment has deposited in blacks' collective psyche some deep and painful scars that still exist today. And worst of all many blacks have been programmed to hate themselves. Many do not like their skin tone or color. They cannot accept their broad nose and coarse hair. In fact, there are those who either perm their hair to look more European or cut it bald to hide it.

On a daily basis, minorities have negative experiences that have caused them to be tried unjustly in the court systems. Therefore, many blacks have been made to feel ashamed of who they are and where they've come from. Even in the black church, they have requested that the "Lord, wash them whiter than snow." America's greatest musical artist, Michael Jackson, who recently died, chemically relaxed his naturally curly hair to make it stringy and straight as whites. He bleached his skin to lighten his natural color to look porcelain white. He has played favoritism toward white children and resented, at times, the blue-black African American. Yet, he claimed in an earlier recording that it doesn't matter if you're black or white.

Now that we know that the Lord is on our side, we can deal with the numerous oppressions, injustices, centuries of being enslaved, segregation by Jim Crow, as well as being ostracized, despised, ghettoized and criticized. We have suffered much! Yet, the miracle has always been the Lord was on our side.

The reason why the Lord is on our side is because, as James Cone, the "Father of Black Theology", suggests, "God is always on the side of the oppressed not the oppressor." He is the God of the oppressed! The reason why He is on the side of the oppressed is because He was oppressed. Jesus was despised and rejected. He was not on the side of the power structure, but He was committed to transforming it. And like some black males, He got into trouble with the law. One of His disciples even became a government informant and turned Him over to the authorities. He, like many of our black men, was arrested without being told the nature of the charges levied against Him or which law was broken and what crime He had committed. He was beaten while in jail under the Roman soldiers' command. Jesus was tried without a lawyer or jury. In fact, Jesus was found guilty even before He was arrested. They even planted evidence on Him that was not there when He said He was a king. He was arguing that His kingdom was not of this world and that He was not a king of this world. They tried Him five times without the presence of a lawyer in four courts and he didn't get justice in any of them.

They released a known criminal who had been found guilty in a trial by a jury so they could be able to have a crucifix available on which to hang Him.

Like Rodney King, Jesus was a victim of police brutality. For the Bible says that the authorities whipped Him all night long.

It is easy to recognize that it was an awful miscarriage of justice Jesus experienced prior to the crucifixion. But we now know why the Lord is on our side. It is because He knows what we go through here in America with this "Justice" system. Many know the miscarriage of justice. But as the song writer said, *I'm so glad that trouble don't last always.* and *The Lord is on our side,* and as Genesis 18:25 states, 'One day the God of all the earth shall do right.' Justice is coming, and prayerfully mixed with grace and mercy to those who have corrected the injustices in America.

RELEASED BY THE LORD
The Day the Victim Becomes the Victor

CHAPTER 17

Nelson Rolihlahia Mandela, a son of the Tembu tribe of Umtata, became a lawyer and a member of the African National Congress. He knew that apartheid was wrong in South Africa and fought against it. Mandela was arrested in August 1962 for treason and sentenced to life imprisonment in June 1964 for sabotage and treason. Although he was innocent of both counts and framed for treason, Mandela spent over twenty-seven years in prison. In February 1990, President F.W. DeKlerk released Mandela from prison and he became the president of South Africa. Had Mandela lived under the Americanized justice system would it had made much difference?

LIFE LESSONS YOU CAN TAKE AWAY FROM THIS STORY

Many believe that America has always been the greatest example of a free, equal and fair society. It is true that our society was built upon moral codes of ethics with freedom of expression, freedom of thought, and freedom of religion and equality toward all. Yet, America is well known for the ways in which she punishes her criminals to deter unlawful conduct and to administer its laws to protect all the people. The system we are describing is the justice system as we know it here in the United States of America. It is a system that makes our country unique and great and can be used to encourage humane behavior and life.

When we think of the justice system we think of those scales of justice as described earlier. Justice ought to be equally balanced at all times toward all people in order to assure equality and fairness for all regardless of skin color, texture of hair or thickness of lips. These symbols of justice can be seen in every courtroom of every state in America and are displayed within the U.S. Supreme Court. Yet, when reading the conclusion as it relates to the story of Nelson Mandela, it still begs the question: Is justice *just* right for all or is it an unfair system built *just* for some people?

Before analyzing this, we must gather a clearer understanding of the Americanized justice system. Our justice system includes the idea of fairness, moral rightness and equity that ought to conform to right action and attitude in its judgments. It is then that those who administer laws ought to reward and punish based on similar actions.

We, here in America, have become extremely proud of the idea of justice when we think of humane intentions to do right towards all humans and to protect each other from violent behavior. However, before extending our chest and raising our shoulders in a proud boast of America's justice system, we must take a closer look at how our legal system and society may have failed us in its principles and practices.

It is assumed that justice is for all. And based upon Mandela's life, if he lived in America under similar circumstances, it is presumed that justice would have be dispensed toward all equally when in reality it may not.

The beauty of America is that we live in a multi-cultural society that proudly reminds us that America is a melting pot for everyone. Yet, we see an array of cultures, races and religions being abused today, such as the Mexicans in Arizona. Notwithstanding, we still find groups of people who seem not to be able to "melt" in the pot. They have been here for nearly 400 years. "Who are these people?" you may ask. They are African Americans, the historical Negro of the past, who have connected themselves to historical blacks in both Africa and America. They are African Americans who have survived the greatest injustices in world history, compared to their European counterparts, in the form of American slavery. I emphasize "American Slavery" for there has never been a kind of oppression and enslavement in the world as America's.

From the very beginning, America has been surrounded in clouds of hypocrisy. Justice Thurgood Marshall once said, "What is striking is the role legal principles have played throughout America's history in determining the condition of Negroes. They were enslaved by law, emancipated by law, disenfranchised and segregated by law; and, finally, they have begun to win equality by law." Sadly, we must admit that the truth of the Declaration of Independence was a lie to black people. In the Declaration, all men are created equal but the Supreme Court issued its *Dred Scott* decision in 1857 that nullified the statement of the Declaration of Independence. One of the main questions addressed in this case was whether a black slave could sue for his or her freedom, and the answer of the Court was 'no.' When the preamble of the Constitution attempted to affirm the inclusiveness of its declaration which begins "*We the People*," Chief Justice Taney who looked at the negative history of black people as an African American stated, "*We think they are not, and that they are not included, and were not intended to be included... They had for more than a century before been regarded as beings of an inferior order, and altogether unfit to associate with the white race...a Negro of the African race was regarded...as an article of property, and held, and bought and sold as such.*"

And what the *Dred Scott* decision did to major documents that affirmed equality was to cancel them out by alleging that black people were not "people" but property that whites had a right to enjoy and be entertained by in both free and slave states. This ideology still, in a lesser degree, remains a kind of cornerstone in the mind and action of many American lawmakers.

It is a shame that people of African descent have had to

fight many battles to be recognized as "people" and "humans." Shamefully, as one law was declared unconstitutional, another law was added to further dehumanize black people in America. For example, everyone knows that soon after the Fourteenth Amendment was passed in 1868 and ratified, those "separate but equal" laws, the Supreme Court in 1896 did another interpretation of the law in *Plessey v. Ferguson to* reaffirm oppression of black people as *"separate and unequal"* in reality. This became "the law" for the next sixty or so years in America's justice system. Again, black people were "no people" in America.

When the Supreme Court declared in *Plessey* that it was constitutional for states to pass laws segregating people solely on the basis of race, mandatory segregation became the law of the land. Furthermore, the *Jim Crow* segregation laws of separate but unequal as defined by the *1896 Plessey v. Ferguson* Supreme Court decision, was one of the worst decisions of the U.S. Supreme Court in this country. It reinforced inequities like never before though some would argue they did this out of ignorance. Suddenly, separate schools controlled by white officials could decide on how little should be spent, what could be taught, and what type of subservient teachers could deliver the educational instructions to black children. School boards were then allowed to spend two to ten times more on white children's education than on Black children. The Black schools had few operational buildings and equipment with no mandatory attendance, and historically often remained closed during the seasons of planting and harvest. Often, the Black school term was shortened. Segregation led to an inferior health care system for Black people. Public hospitals supported by public funds even turned away Black patients due to legalized segregation.

The spread of legalized segregation led to many Negroes becoming and remaining, even to this day, a kind of second-class citizen and life. The legal system was bad for those Negroes living under Jim Crow segregation laws but its impact could be even worse for some in the 21st century. Although the Negro, during earlier times, traveled in third-class accommodations for first-class fare and lived in neighborhoods filled with crime with little attention to services such as sewers, street lighting, or roads, many African Americans today exist with no health care or employment. Many in the urban centers today don't have money to pay their utility bills to keep the lights or water on or purchase a home and even send their children to top rated schools.

Malcolm X's conclusion in the 1960's regarding the "American dream", termed by Martin Luther King in 1963 is still today for many blacks, an "American nightmare." "The law", as Thurgood Marshall labeled it, has and continues to have a powerful negative impact on the basic civil rights of black people. Today, injustice in the law still has a way of destroying many Black Americans. The question of whether injustice is *just* for us is not a moot point for those of us who are "the people of the oppressed" as James Cone terms it. I think if you are black in America there is limited justice and perhaps, still to some, no justice at all.

I SHALL NOT FEAR
The Lord is With Me

CHAPTER 18

And when Elijah saw how things were, he ran for his dear life.

—I Kings 19:3a

Some years ago, the story was told there was a village in the Ukraine where a man was found in a barn, in a ghost-like condition. He looked like he hadn't taken a bath in years. He was dirty, nasty looking, and smelling. Terror, fear, and fright flashed on his face when he was discovered in the barn and for forty-one of his seventy-four years of life he had lived in this barn in that condition.

What was discovered is this: This man had been a Russian soldier during World War I, and after just one brief day, he had joined the invading German army. The Nazis had allowed him to return home, where he lived peacefully until a Soviet or Russian army recaptured the territory in 1944. Afraid that his Russian countrymen would punish him as a traitor, for his earlier surrender to the Nazis, he disappeared into his barn for some forty-one years, threatening to kill his wife if she betrayed him or told his whereabouts.

She protected him for forty-one years by not allowing visitors to come to their house, locking the house whenever she left for work at a nearby farm. Three times a day, she shoved food to him through a make shift hole in the barn's wall. And most of the neighbors thought he, like the other thousands of soldiers, was dead or missing in action. And only once did this man leave the barn, and at that time he did so by dressing up in women's clothing, but he became so frightened that day he ran back to his shelter, and never ventured out again. He was not discovered until his wife died and the neighbors came to go through her belongings.

When the authorities found this man, instead of punishing him, they realized they could not have invented any torture that would match the hell and fear that he had created for himself, so they just let him go. My, how this soldier handled his fear.

Another story is told about how years ago there was a well-known TV circus show featuring Bengal tigers and a trainer. While the show was going on, an electrical storm turned the lights out. For twenty or thirty long minutes, the trainer was locked in the cage with giant tigers, a whip and chair in hand. Those in the audience thought the trainer would be mulled and when the lights came on he was alright. The next day, at a TV interview the trainer was asked, "How did you survive?" He said, "I kept cracking my whips and holding up the chair, even though I couldn't see the tigers –they could both hear the whips in the dark, and see the chair. They never knew that I couldn't see them." God shows us how to handle our fears.

LIFE LESSONS YOU CAN TAKE AWAY FROM THIS STORY

Elijah, the Prophet is the main character in this text. And what the Prophet teaches us is, how to handle our fears. Elijah is that Prophet who seldom shows up in Biblical history. But when he does, it does us all well to take note of him. We ought to listen and learn not only from what he does, but also from what he says because when he shows up, he seldom says a lot. He is a man of few words, yet his words are very powerful. On one occasion he shows up briefly and just says, "Why halt ye between two opinions? if the Lord be God, serve Him. But if Baal, then follow him!" Elijah kind of comes and goes. So watch him when he does show up.

History calls him, "The Chief of Prophets," not because he wrote a whole lot of books, but because of what he says and does. If you want to follow a person of great stature, don't just read what they say, but watch what they do. There is an old adage that goes like this: I'd rather "See" a Sermon, than "Hear" one. Elijah's life is meaningful and so is his walk and talk.

181

So great was his prayer, that on this occasion, he prayed down fire from Heaven that burned up 450 prophets of Baal and their altar. And it's out of this context, that Ahab, the king, tells Jezebel, the Queen, and she puts a bounty on his head and swears that Elijah will be dead within twenty-four hours.

Elijah the prophet is afraid and fears for his life. If the truth is told, most of us have some kind of fear. We are afraid of something. We are afraid of the loss of a loved one. Have you felt the dread of hearing those words on the phone, or being at the hospital to hear those dreaded words: "I am sorry to inform you..." Or, what parent hasn't walked the floor at night when their son or daughter didn't come home in time, thinking, "Something must have happened to them."

Death scares us and so does divorce. If you've been through a divorce you know it's much like a death the moment one of the two says, "I just don't love you anymore. I want out. This marriage has been dead for a long time." Those words sound so much like, "I'm sorry to inform you...." We are afraid of the loss of things that we value such as our houses! One week a tornado touched down and one lady lost it all and said, "I don't know how I can go on. I've lost everything!" Not quite so – she DID NOT LOSE her life! Buddha is quoted as saying: "The Less you have, the Less you have to worry about." Jesus said, *"Do not store up for yourselves treasures on earth, But store up for yourselves treasures in heaven..."* (Matt. 6:19-21). Some of us are afraid of being found out!

But there is this thing called "Imposter Syndrome." Seventy percent of all successful individuals are afraid. Most of us are afraid of something!

However, Elijah in a few words, tells us how to handle our fears. In the Scriptures, Ahab calls him, "The Troubler of Israel" because of the destruction of the 450 Prophets of Baal. Queen Jezebel has made him "A Fugitive in Israel." He runs and hides himself in a cave. Now he is not the only one who has ever experienced fear:

> Moses feared and fled to the Midian Desert, after committing first degree murder of an Egyptian and stayed there for forty years.

> David feared and found shelter at Engedi when King Saul pursued his life.

> John feared and was abandoned on the Isle of Patmos to prevent his persecution.

> Martin Luther, out of fear, took refuge from his enemies at the Castle of Wartburg.

> Martin Luther King feared and found refuge in a Memphis Church, Mason Temple, and gave the *Been to the Mountaintop Speech,* running from a country that turned against him after giving a Speech against

the Vietnam War.

And if you live long enough, some kind of fear will grip you. But Elijah tells us how to handle our fear!

The first thing he tells us is don't panic. A whole lot of folk mess up and lose it all just because they panic. In the city of Twinsburg, Ohio, it is reported that a man named Lamar shot and killed Twinsburg policeman, Josh Miktarian. He said, he was afraid and grabbed the policeman's gun, shot him in the head, and then three more times. What happened? He panicked. Elijah says to us, "Don't Panic." When you can't sleep, the Psalmist says instead of counting sheep, count on the Shepherd. The Twenty-Third Psalm says, *"The Lord is my shepherd....yea though I walk through the valley of the shadow of death, I will not fear."*

Second, Elijah says in I Kings 19:9, if you fear, make sure you run to the right place. He says, he starts at Mt. Carmel and runs to Mt. Horeb which is interpreted, "The Mount of the Lord."

Third, never forget to pray through until you get a breakthrough. Elijah didn't stop praying until he got a breakthrough or a word from the Lord and encouragement to continue his journey. When Elijah was in the cave, God assured him that he was not alone and said to him, "I got 7,000 who have yet to bow their knees to Baal." We all have got to learn to pray until God comes through in some kind of breakthrough.

Joshua did and after seven days of praying, the walls of Jericho came down.

Shadrach, Meshach and Abednego did, and a fourth person showed up in the furnace.

Job did and said, "All my appointed days, I will wait till a change comes."

So when you are afraid, don't panic and hide in a barn for some forty-one years or crack your whip in a lion's cage. What you need to do is run to God, seek His face and wait on Him until He gives you an answer; until you get a breakthrough.

THE POINT OF NO RETURN
You are Never Alone

CHAPTER 19

I have been given complete authority in heaven and on earth.
—Jesus Christ, Matthew 28:18

I'm reminded of a story about a brother by the name of Erskie Jenkins. He was a prominent businessman in the city. He was known for his money, his cars, and his so-called status. And he was also a member of the CET pack. You know, the CET pack. They observe the church three times a year: Christmas, Easter, and Thanksgiving. And on that one or two days a year when he made it to church, he would sit in the same seat down front and to the left, cross his legs and read the news from his cell phone. And when it was offering time he always gives a $100 bill in a braggadocios manner.

So after his usual once a year journey to the house of God, he goes about his business as usual. But a few weeks later old Erskie took sick. He was diagnosed with a rare sickness, and was out of commission for weeks. Erskie, being a rich and influential man, told his assistants, accountants, and lawyers to bring the following people to his bedside to see if they could heal him. So he had his assistant call Mother Williams. He said, "Bring me Mother Williams. When the pastor does his thing at church, I always see Mother Williams dancing and shouting like she's dancing with the stars." He thought to himself, "Maybe she can pray over me and dance in my room and I can be healed." Then he said, "Bring Brother Jakes—that TV preacher, I love watching him preach that sermon called "Junk in the Trunk", and maybe that's why I feel so bad, I got junk in my trunk and maybe he can help me clear some things up in my life." He further requested, "Bring that preacher Mr. Joel in. I love listening to him and his 'feel good' message, because he helps me realize how perfect I am." And, then he said lastly, "Bring me Pastor Macon. Although I support him once a year, visit him once a year, and don't even listen to what he tells me to do with my life, I still want him here."

So the four of them came and did their thing. Mother Williams did her dance and the great Bishop Jakes came and preached about getting the junk out of his trunk. Mr. Joel Osteen told him to enjoy his journey called life, and be kind to the garbage man when he picks up your trash. And Pastor Macon even stopped by to throw a prayer of healing up for brother Erskie. And, he actually was healed from his sickness, but he went back to his old ways.

However, three months later Erskie took sick again and died. This time he was really upset. He made it to the pearly white gates of Heaven, and in a stern manner he looked to the angels and said, "Reservations for Erskie Jenkins. I should be near the front. I gave my church $100 per holiday." The angel looked at him and smiled, and said, "O.k. Sir, one moment." As the angel was looking for his name, brother Jenkins said, "And when you find my name I need to speak to God and Jesus right away. It's a private matter, but I need Father and Son right away."

Well, the angel found his name and said, "Here it is! I didn't find you at the top of the list, but you're on the list nonetheless, so come right in. I will see if God and Jesus will see you." So later he got his appointment and he asked God, "Our Heavenly Father, why did you let me leave so early? I had so many things left to do. I felt cheated." He said, " Why, I only was sick one time this year, and was healed. Then the second time I just died instantly. Why didn't you help a brother out?"

Well, God said, "I figured since you visited my house one time a year, I would visit yours once a year and that was good enough too!" Today, I'd like to ask the question, "What do you do when you've reached the point of no return?"

LIFE LESSONS YOU CAN TAKE AWAY FROM THIS STORY

I have found out that there are times in our lives when we feel like we have reached a point of no return. When I think of that expression, I look to the definition which says that, "The point of no return is the point beyond which someone, or some group of people must continue on their current course of action, either because turning back is physically impossible, or because to turn back would be too expensive or dangerous."

This term is also used in aviation and it is characterized with the acronym of PNR, which let's the pilot know that on a particular flight, due to fuel consumption, a plane is no longer capable of returning to its airfield of original takeoff. After passing this particular point, the pilot has no option but to continue to some other destination. He is now subject to an irrevocable commitment. A choice of moving forward in the right direction, or steering back into a bad place.

Isn't that like life? There are times when we find ourselves in situations where the fuel has been used, the money has been spent, the favors have run out, brother or sister who used to bail us out is no longer answering the phone—we are now barraged with a serious choice.

I was reading a book the other day called the *Secrets to Making Great Decisions* and the first thing it says you ought to do if you want to become a great decision maker is you have to first decide if you have a choice. If you don't, then you don't have to waste your time deciding anything. But if you do have a choice or a decision to make, if there is a right way and a wrong way, if there is a rough path or an easy path, then what do you do when you get yourself in a situation where you have to move forward and turning back is no longer a viable option?

What do you do when you have moved from the honeymoon period of this thing called life, into the "real world" where temptations, problems, troubles, storms, people talking about you, friends leaving you, and endless tribulation are the order of the day? It is those moments when you look in the mirror and you say to yourself, "I don't know how I got here, things were fine just a few months ago. I never thought I'd find myself feeling this way. I don't know where I'm headed. I seem to have lost my way." But just as you ask that question, your faith muscles kick in and you leave the earthly mindset and let the spirit take over and you come to the realization that somehow somebody bigger than you and me helped you get here, and that same somebody can help you get to where you need to be.

I don't know who I'm talking to, but somebody looked in that mirror and said, *I've come this far by faith. Leaning on the Lord. Trusting in His Holy Word. He's never failed me yet.* Somebody has been to the point of no return.

I'm reminded of the story of four people who were on a plane together and an hour into the plane ride the pilot announced that the plane was going down and that in order to be saved they all would have to jump. Then after letting everybody know the situation, the pilot put on his parachute and jumped out the plane leaving only three parachutes for the four passengers.

The first passenger to grab a parachute was a doctor who explained that he was on the verge of discovering a cure for cancer; therefore, he was clearly the most important passenger. So he quickly put the parachute on his back and jumped out of the doomed plane. The second passenger claimed to be the smartest man in the world. "Surely you wouldn't want the smartest man in the world to go down with this plane," he explained. So he quickly picked up something and jumped out the plane. Then the only two passengers left were a Boy Scout and a minister. The minister told the young boy that he had lived a good life and was ready to die, so the boy should take the parachute and jump to safety. The Boy Scout calmly answered the minister and said, "Don't worry, there are still two parachutes left. The smartest man in the world just jumped out the plane with my backpack."

It's evident that in this life nobody is as smart as they think they are. You may have degree one, two, and three or position low, medium, and high, but like that old saying "I just can't do this thing called life by myself. I can't do it alone. I need somebody bigger than my situation, somebody bigger than my enemy, somebody bigger than my doctor and somebody bigger than my lawyer." There's a saying that says "Jesus, take the wheel cause I'm at a point where I can't drive this road by myself. But one thing I do know is, that I am not turning back cause I'm at a point in my life where turning back is not an option. I'm at a point of no return."

Here in the text, Jesus has reached a pivotal point in the realization of His earthly purpose and His Father's plan. Look back and paint the picture: Jesus being led out to be killed and a heavy untreated wooden cross is thrown on His shoulders and He accepts it. The cross is thrust into His arms, and the King of kings is ordered to carry it to the site of His execution. Picture Him as He is on His way to the hill of the skull, known as Golgotha, to be crucified between two guilty men. Yet, He is not guilty of anything. Oh, it's a rough situation when you are being crucified for something you did not do. It's a rough spot when people think they know who you are when they really don't know you from Adam.

Jesus is beaten. He is mocked. And He is bent over from the heavy weight. He's bleeding. Picture the pain He must have endured. It was so painful that even His captors probably had to close their hearts and minds so as to not feel it themselves. Then verse forty-five says that there was three hours of darkness over the land. Some of us can't stand three minutes in a dark hour let alone three hours. The uninterrupted episodes of darkness was no commercial and our afflicted Savior is at a pivotal point. Has anybody ever been in any darkness? There are definitely more people scared of the dark than the light. But know today, that the natural way of God's plan is that darkness has to give way to the light. Know today, that because of the fact that Jesus carried the cross for you and me, your darkness won't last always. Jesus encountered darkness on the cross so that the darkness of your past would not be the inevitable fate of the future.

Then, later in the text it says, He let life go. He let go for you and me. If He had not yielded, where would we be? Even though He did no wrong, He allowed the darkness to overtake His inevitable light, for a moment, for you and for me. My God allowed the breath of life to leave His Son so that we don't have to be swallowed up in the trenches of sin and so that we can live life more abundantly.

One Bible translation says He gave up His ghost so that the ghost of our inevitable sin would not be our inevitable future. And when you reference the story about the price that Jesus paid for you, you will have comfort in knowing that in your own life, some things aren't meant to change, but are meant to survive. If you can't alter it, just out-live it because the price has already been paid. Jesus died for you and me. And because He paid the price, I now have a refuge and some strength and help when I'm in trouble. And because He paid the price, even when I walk through some valleys and see mountains to climb in my life, I will fear no evil because my God is with me. Thy rod and thy staff comfort me.

So when life gets hard on your back and you don't have to make a permanent decision based on a temporary circumstance, your answer may be delayed, but it's not denied. Somebody once said that you got to have patience and patience is like a tree whose root is bitter, but its fruit is sweet.

And I've come here to tell you that nothing the enemy does to you can abort the plan that God has for your life.

Somebody here today is wrestling with something that they have no business even giving attention to, because my Bible says that the battle is not yours; it's the Lord's. And, if it's the Lord's, that tells me that it's the truth. I remember Martin Luther King saying, "That truth crushed down to the ground will rise again undaunted." And Jesus is the Way, the Truth, and the Life, and that tells me that when they persecuted my God, when they mocked Him, even when they nailed Him to the cross, they could not hide the Truth. So if the Truth can't be hidden, then that means it will set you free. So that tells me, when you are all alone and you're at a point where you feel that all hope is gone and things seem impossible, don't you worry, because my Bible says that, "God knows how to make all things work together for good to them that love the Lord." Also, my Bible says, "Weeping may endure for a night. But night time won't be your portion always." Nothing can separate us from the protection of JESUS.

Somebody is struggling with finding out the outcome of your destiny. But know today that God is a God of order. He does things by appointment. And the good thing about appointments is that it is already set up. It's got a time. It's got a name. It's got a date. It's got a location. It's like GPS - the distance, date, and time is right on point!

So your blessing already has an appointment. Your miracle already has an appointment. David said, "My time is in thy hand." See, you got to talk to God. It's like the song, you've got to say, *It's Me, It's Me, It's Me, Oh, Lord, standing in the need of prayer.* And how can you ask anything of anyone you don't talk to? Some of us have got to communicate to God. So you say, "What does that mean to me?" Well, it means that when you hit that point of life where you feel like you want to turn back, the point when you know that because of the sacrifice, because of the darkness He encountered, that your worldly defeat is not your planned destiny!

So when you are down and out and there seems like there's nowhere to run and you feel like the rich young ruler in Luke eighteen, saying, "Master, what must I do?" Just think back to the story of Noah where it says, "But God remembered me."

Is there anybody who knows that God remembered you? And, if God remembered you, you do have something to shout about! If God has ever looked beyond your faults and delivered you regardless of what you used to be, you do have something to shout about.

Is there anybody in this house who has felt the work of the Lord even before your eyes could see it? In Job 23, it says, "Behold, I go forward, but I couldn't see him there. I went back and I still couldn't see Him. I know he's putting in work on my left side, but I still didn't see it. He hideth Himself on the right hand that I cannot see him." But the good part is the verse goes on and says, "But He knows the way that I take. He sees me wherever I go." If God knows where you are; and if you can just look back over your shoulder at your past and see where He brought you from, somebody knows that the hand of the Lord has been on you all your life. And even when you feel like all hope was gone, you should have something to shout about because even Jesus asked the question, "My God, My God, why hath thou forsaken me?" He may have questioned God's acts, but he never questioned His relationship with Him.

Hold on to your relationship with God…just like the song says: *Ain't no stopping us now, we're on the move.* And in your hour of crisis, when you hit that point of no return, many of us search for the place of rest rather than for the answer. But,

- If I can find God, I don't need to find money.
- If I can find God, I don't need to find healing.
- If I can find God, I don't need to find significance.
- If I can find God, I don't need to find position.
- If I can find God, I don't need to rely on that man.
- If I can find God, I don't have to rely on that woman.
- If I can find God, my needs are no longer needs.
- If I can find God, my struggle is no longer a struggle.
- If I can find God, my pain is no longer pain.

And when you wave your situation in the light of His presence, then, "There is no secret what God CAN DO" because what is a problem if God is there? You don't need a healing, you need a healer. You don't just need the act of God, you just need the presence of God.

The Bible says in Matthew 28:18, "And Jesus came and spoke saying, all authority has been given to me in heaven and on earth." And later, in verse twenty, it says, *"And lo, I am with you always even to the end of the age."* And if you ever get to a point in your life where you feel like you are all alone, or you don't have all you need to continue on, never forget that He is with you "even to the end." The great thing about the translation of that text, "to the end", is, it means to the consummation or to the entire completion.

So when you feel like you're at a point of no return, know that you can find ease in moving forward with the One Who died for you—Jesus Christ. There's a song that says, *Jesus paid it all. All to Him I owe. Sin had left a crimson stain. He washed me white as snow.*

THE DAY I WAS CHALLENGED
Don't Magnify the Problem - Magnify Your God

CHAPTER 20

I remember when I was in High School, I had a challenge that would change the way that I looked at life forever. I grew up playing sports; football was my thing and I loved doing it. I believed that one day I would be a great athlete and would go to college on a full scholarship.

As time went on, I got to my junior year of football, which was the year that most colleges look at the athletes and at that time I was so far from a college prospect I didn't even think about a college draft. I played on a team that only won three games, (I think in its whole history), but at least for the past season. I spent most of the season injured, and we had no one coming to the games, not even the flies.

The next year was not looking any brighter, we had barely any returning starters, the head coach had resigned and all of the newspapers picked my team to be last in the division. We were the laughing stock of the high school league.

As a former injured player, I didn't know what to do. All

I thought about before the season was going to another school. I didn't care if it was in Alaska; I just knew there wouldn't be a victory coming for the Nordornia Knights. That was the name of my team because they thought they were shining knights in armor. They had more nights than armor because every thing was always bleak for them. And, boy, was I complaining about being on the team outside of Cleveland that was at one time called the "Mistake on the Lake." I knew if I played for my high school team the mistake would have extended outside of my school life.

Any how, one day I decided to ask my father about the situation and what he thought, and he told me that any mistake could be corrected. He even got churchy with me. I remember him saying, "Son, believe in the Lord your God, and He will bring you victory. Do not magnify your problems, but magnify your God." Boy, was I changed! I never heard it like that before, but I really started believing. In the morning, I believed. In the noon, I started believing. Before I went to bed, I believed. Why, I believed so much until I think even Lebron James, the former Cleveland Cav basketball player became a witness. I was changed from that moment on. I was no longer stagnant, but I started to believe and move from a victim to a victor. From then on, I was filled with the Spirit of the Lord and let Him lead my footsteps and what happened next was nothing short of a miracle.

That season I gave it all I had and ended up being captain of the team. Why, I even led the team all the way to the State

Championship and we won the division. I thought my name was changed from Daniel the football player, to David the challenger of the giant Goliath. What everybody else thought of my team was now being challenged by a higher perception. They didn't know what was happening, but I knew God was in control! I was so good until some college scouts saw me play, pray, and heard me say, "We are the Best" and gave me a full scholarship to a Division One College.

It all started from a small inspirational word from my dad who just told me, "Don't magnify your problems, but magnify your God" and that's when I started to progress. I'm just glad I had a dad who made me glad and not sad!

LIFE LESSONS YOU CAN TAKE AWAY FROM THIS STORY

There are many times in life where God has said something to us and had something for us to do and yet we found ourselves defeated. There are battles in life that God wants to help us win, people He wants us to help save and even favors He wants to give to us, but in many cases we can't even see the playing field. And you cannot do it if you are not progressing, or moving forward and most of all, trusting God to diminish your problems and accentuate His favor. I am sure the enemy has been trying to weigh you down. Well, I want to push you; I want to beat down the line of the enemy's stronghold in your life. I want you to break free of all those things that are holding you in bondage so that you can attain all that God has for you now and in your future!

Nobody likes unnecessary pain, worry, or strains. It's time to make a declaration like I did on the day I talked to my father. You have to say, "I may be down right now but I'm going to be great tomorrow. I may be in famine right now but I'm going some place in my life. I am moving forward!" Hebrews 11:32 says, "I do not have time to tell about Gideon, Barak, Samson, Jephthah..." Who is Jephthah? All of the others are familiar names in the Bible but who is that last individual, and what did he do to earn a spot in the Bible Hall of Fame?

Let me tell you who Jephthah was in the Bible. Jephthah was one of the great military heroes in Israel's history. But to get to that point of greatness it took him going through a rough road and time in his life. His family life was rough: his mom was a prostitute, his dad was promiscuous, and his half brothers were hateful and threw him out of the house. He tried to turn to the leadership of the city fathers, the one group of people who he thought he could depend on, and they played politics and turned their backs on him.

But even though Jephthah may have been broken, he was certainly not defeated. The Bible says this man, out of devastation, found direction for his life and you can do the same! Jephthah was a man who lived in a cave but refused to live like a victim. Even though he was going through a lot, he decided to prepare for his future. He decided to move forward. So he recruited and trained an army. And one day Israel was attacked and the city's fathers ran to him for help. These were the same men who played party politics against him when he came to them earlier for help.

What would you have done? Would you have refused to help them in their time of need? Or would you go out of your way and put your life on the line for individuals who played games with you? Well, Jephthah put his life on the line for them! By doing so, he earned himself a spot in the Bible next to Gideon, Barak, and Samson.

So, today, whatever you are going through or been through, I want you to know that God wants to magnify Himself in your life, in your problems and through your situations. What's your excuse for not moving forward? Jephthah refused to let his past rob him of his promising future. Instead of curling up in self-pity, he rose up and took control.

How did he do it? I can tell you because I've been through it. He did it by observing three life changing principles.

The first thing he did was **he let go of his past.** To move forward in your life it is absolutely essential that you let go of your past so that you can gain a great future. There's a step beyond death that's called burial and it separates the dead from the living. This is also symbolic of our past and our future. In life, we find people who get past the burial process faster than others and some who never truly do. The key to burying your past is to stop dwelling on the past. If you don't, it will stop you from living in the present.

Do you know anyone who is constantly talking about the past? They continue to talk about what they did back when. It is probably because they are not doing anything right now. When I played football in college, I would always find players who would talk about what they did in high school or how they were such a great player, and how they had the best statistics. What I found out was that most of the college players who talked about High School all the time, weren't really achieving anything on the college level. So they constantly looked back because they weren't currently doing anything. They needed to start playing at a higher level at some point in their lives.

Anytime you speak of the past as if it is the present, it is because you have allowed the past to rob the present right out of your hands. Don't do it! Rise up, and take it back. Don't speak on what no one can change. But plan for the future on the things that you have the power to change.

Furthermore, remember that **purpose is everything**. When you find yourself in pain, you must remember the answer is to have purpose in your life. Many people attempt to find the answer in temporary pleasures such as money, drugs, or even relationships. But the key is to have purpose. If you are battling loneliness or depression, the first step out of it is to find a cause greater than yourself, and give yourself to it. When your focus changes from yourself to others, then your life will take a swing upward. In life, don't be so self-centered; make others your priority.

There is a story told of the late great President Theodore Roosevelt. In an interview, Theodore Roosevelt's son described how his father knew his value. "Father Teddy always had to be the center of attention," said the son. "When he went to a wedding, he wanted to be the bride. When he went to a funeral, he was sad that he couldn't be the corpse!" Don't be so self-centered; you don't have to always be the life of the party.

In High School, during my junior year, I thought about leaving the team. At that point, I was making no progress. It was when I started thinking about rallying the team together that I started making true progress towards being the captain, and a champion.

Moreover, **commit to walking in love and forgiveness.** One day, Peter said to Jesus, "Lord, how often shall my brother sin against me and I forgive him? Till seven times?" Jesus replied, "Until seventy times seven." If you are awake sixteen hours in a day that means forgiving every two minutes! That shows how adamant Jesus was about forgiveness. He constantly urged people to love and forgive. That is true progress.

During the last days when the Berlin Wall was still standing, a garbage man drove a truck full of garbage and poured it onto the other side. Another wiser man on the other side drove a truck full of food and humanitarian aid and left a note that read, "Each gives what he has to give." So, if garbage is what you got, garbage is what you will give. If love and forgiveness is what you got, love and forgiveness will be what you give. What do you have on the inside of you? Do you have garbage, or do you have love? Are you polluting children's lives or your friends' lives? Or are you being the salt of the earth and light for the city that you are called to?

I remember watching Kobe Bryant play in a great NBA game. He had gotten in an altercation with another player. The other player just kept on talking the whole game, because a "big mouth" and "trash talk" is what he had to give. Kobe Bryant just kept scoring, because "skill" is what he was full of. Each person gives what he has to give. Kobe had skill while the other had lip. The trick of the enemy is to get you to lose your progress, but you must choose to keep moving forward today! What do you have on the inside of you? Do you choose to magnify your problems or magnify your God? The choice is yours. Furthermore, your future depends on it. You got to make the right choice! I am a witness that the right choice can make you a champion. You must believe that God is not finished with you yet. This is a concept that I grabbed at an early age, and it will benefit young people to understand it early. And there are older people who need to understand it quickly!

Why waste another moment of your life living in the past? Commit yourselves today to keep moving forward! It is my prayer for all to live in a season of blessing. I pray today that you will live beyond your education, beyond your training, beyond your present state, beyond your past! I pray that you are blessed going in and blessed going out. Opportunity is coming your way, and your faith is rising up. Where the door was shut, it will now be open; where you have been weak, you will be made strong; and where you have been in famine, you will have plenty. In the name of Jesus!

Epilogue

EPILOGUE

A GREAT NATION IS STILL IN THE MAKING

Most of us know of the Jewish captives in the Bible known as the three Hebrew boys: Shadrach, Meshach, and Abednego. The king made a request that every person in the kingdom bow down and worship his golden image at the appropriate time. These three boys refused to obey his orders. When the king heard the response of the Hebrew boys, he ordered that the furnace be heated seven times hotter than normal. Then he sent Shadrach, Meshach, and Abednego to what he believed was certain death. But God took the heat out of the flames. What the king saw when he looked into the furnace was not three men bound but four persons walking around. The fourth had the appearance of the Son of God. Though the three Hebrew boys were let out of the furnace under the orders of the king, the Lord, while walking in the furnace ready to make a great nation of Israel, released them.

When America was faced with the fiery furnaces of these

209

experiences in her history, the Lord has always been with her ready to give release and relief. This is indeed a great nation to live in even through her many historical challenges. However, there comes a time when we must stop blaming others for our plight. We must move away from being the *victim* and take responsibility for our future direction to resolve those issues created by the past. We must believe that our God is able to release us from any and all bondages.

As we look at the story of the three Hebrew boys who were cast into the fiery furnace in Babylon, we must never forget that they, too, were placed into a position of challenge. They, too, were victims of an unjust system under King Nebuchadnezzar. However, these Hebrew brothers believed that God could release them either from the injustices they faced or promote them to a place of freedom and liberation even if it meant death. They trusted in God to release them from the bonds of oppression designed to stymie their physical and spiritual development.

I believe that these men who were placed in the fiery furnace created for themselves a scenario where God was placed in a position where He had to release them because of their faith. Although the king mandated that the fire be increased seven times, the faith of the men were increased seven times as well. They responded to the king how they refused to break the law of God who declared that no other god ought to be worshipped other than the God of Abraham, Isaac and Jacob. Somehow, these who were oppressed, transformed their fiery furnace into a cathedral or a place of worship. The Bible says that there appeared in the furnace a fourth person Who looked like the Son of God. The moment the Son of God showed up, the furnace was transformed into a new place. It became the sanctuary of the living God. I believe that the Hebrew boys learned how to live in a furnace made new.

Again, I say that America, despite its numerous shortcomings, is still one of the best places in the world to live at this time in history for all people. Despite the ever-present spectrum of racism in this country and the illegalities faced by people, Americans are the wealthiest and best-educated people on Earth.

The dilemma of "double-consciousness" to which W.E.B. Dubois referred almost a hundred years ago, is still a frightening reality in the legal system today, and from all indications, the problem of the "color line" will continue to plague us in this twenty-first century. Yet, blacks can achieve success in America, but we must first allow the Lord to give the release. It was the release of the Lord Who enabled those many ancestors to survive hardships much worse than what affects people in America today.

The history of America begins with a group of people who came to this country in search of a release from their slave state. The Pilgrims were motivated by a vision and were willing to do anything to be released from the bondage of the king. America's founding Fathers represent one of the clearest examples of people fulfilling the vision of their ancestors for a release. This nation now stands as the preeminent symbol of freedom and liberty in a world seeking release. This release comes from a real trust in God Who is able to do exceedingly and abundantly all that we ask or think according to His power that works in us!

The three Hebrew boys in the furnace are not aware of the fourth person; only those who were looking from without. The world is now looking upon America and I think they are seeing the fourth person who is with us. God bless America.

WHAT'S YOUR PORCH STORY?

WRITE IT DOWN, NOW!

_____

_____

_____

_____

_____

_____

_____

_____

_____

_____

_____

_____

_____

_____

_____

_____